SHREE MAHAVATAR BABAJI'S SHIVA KRIYA YOGAM

An Introduction to a Way of Life

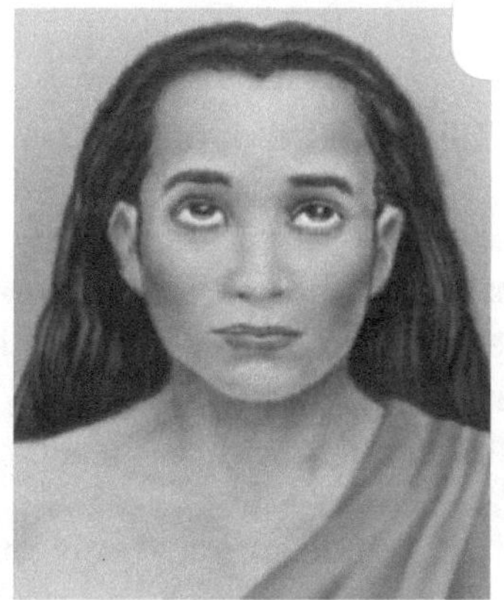

This book presents the teachings of

MAHA KRIYA YOGI SHRI KANDHAGURU IYYA

ISBN 979-8-89699-383-4

Shri Kandhaguru

Eswari

Palanisamy

Chinnaponnu

My first salutations to the divine beings of my heart, who gave birth and nurtured me!

Shri Kandhaguru Iyya

Why This Book?

In a world filled with countless books on Kriya Yogam, you might wonder: Why this book? What makes it different? The answer lies in its simplicity and focus on the beginner's journey.

1. **A Guide for Beginners:** While many books dive deep into advanced philosophies and techniques, few cater to those taking their first steps. This book is designed to bridge that gap, offering a clear and approachable introduction to Kriya Yogam for anyone curious about its transformative potential.
2. **Consolidated Knowledge:** Information about Kriya Yogam is often scattered across various sources, making it challenging to form a comprehensive understanding. This book gathers essential teachings, practices, and insights in one place, providing a cohesive guide for readers.
3. **Accessible Language:** Many existing texts on Kriya Yogam are written in complex, high-level English, which can be intimidating or difficult to grasp for many readers. This book prioritizes clarity and simplicity, ensuring that spiritual wisdom is accessible to everyone, regardless of their proficiency in English.

In essence, this book aims to demystify Kriya Yogam, making it an open door for anyone seeking spiritual growth without the barriers of scattered information or overly sophisticated language.

Before You Begin: A Gentle Introduction

Take a moment. Close your eyes.

Now, take a deep breath.

Do you feel it?

The gentle rhythm of life flowing within you?

Imagine if you could tap into this rhythm more fully, unlocking a profound sense of peace, clarity, and balance. What if there was a way to connect deeply with yourself, releasing stress and finding joy in each moment?

This book is your invitation to explore the world of Kriya Yogam, a practice that can help you discover just that. It's about beginning a conversation between your inner self and the universe.

Here's a glimpse of what you can look forward to on this transformative journey:

What is Kriya Yogam?

We'll introduce you to Kriya Yogam in a way that's simple, warm, and easy to understand.

The Power of the Breath:

You'll discover how your breath is far more than just a biological function. It's a powerful tool to restore inner balance and deepen your connection to your true self.

An Inspiring Story:

You'll meet Mahavatar Babaji, the timeless master who revived Kriya Yogam for the modern world. His story is not just inspiring—it's a reminder that profound transformations are possible for anyone, no matter where you start.

Gentle Steps into Practice:

Worried that you're a beginner? Don't be. This book is designed for you. We'll guide you through gentle, easy-to-follow steps so you can start experiencing the benefits of Kriya Yogam without feeling overwhelmed or pressured.

The Guruji Who Taught Us Kriya Yogam:

Discover the wisdom of the teacher who brought this practice to us and the profound benefits that come with it.

Human Body's Connection with the Universe:

Learn how the human body is not separate but intricately linked to the greater universe. It's a fascinating exploration that will shift the way you see yourself and the world around you.

Karma, Pancha Bhutas, and the Seven Chakras:

We'll explain these ancient concepts in a way that's easy to grasp, showing how they shape your life and your spiritual journey.

Healthy Body and Sound Mind:

Find out how Kriya Yogam helps you maintain a healthy body and a calm, focused mind—essential for living a balanced life.

Cleansing Your Soul:

Discover methods to cleanse not just your body, but your soul as well, helping you release past baggage and cultivate a sense of inner peace.

Revitalizing Blood Cells:

Learn how Kriya Yogam can help you rejuvenate your body from the inside out, supporting healthy blood circulation and overall well-being.

Transforming Yourself:

Experience a total transformation—physically, mentally, and spiritually. Kriya Yogam offers you the tools to become the best version of yourself, awakening your true potential.

And ultimately*, you'll see how all of these powerful lessons come together through the practice of Kriya Yogam, guiding you on a path toward lasting peace, health, and happiness.*

Are you ready to begin this life-changing journey?
With each page, you'll uncover new insights and practices that can lead to the transformation you've been seeking.

This isn't just a book—it's your first step into a more harmonious life.

Author of this Book Based on Guruji's Teachings

Note from the Author

I was born and raised in a middle-class family in Chennai and graduated in Economics from Madras Christian College, Tambaram. My father, Sri IN Murthy, and my mother, Shreemathi Leelavathy, were the foundation of my spiritual journey and fondness for spirituality.

I worked for nearly 33 years with various MNCs before retiring at the age of 62. Throughout different phases of my life, I found myself at crossroads, suffering from numerous ailments and undergoing treatments, none of which led to a cure.

As a strong believer in Shridi Sai Baba, I prayed for guidance to find a Guruji who could teach me spirituality and cleanse my mind. My prayers were answered when I first encountered Kandhaguru Guruji in 2023. Since then, Guruji has taught me Kriya Yogam, and within a year of practicing daily during Brahma Muhurtham, I regained both a healthy body and a sound mind.

Looking back, I realize that the reminder to look inward is truly a call to spiritual awakening. Through inner exploration, I discovered that the divine light I sought was already within me. For a long time, I lived without understanding life's true purpose, caught up in confusion. But I came to see that the human body is a remarkable creation, and we carry a divine spark within us. Each of us has a unique inner wisdom, called Ghaanam, which reveals truths and helps us master life.

Practicing Kriya Yogam helped me unlock this wisdom, guiding me to greater understanding and success. As humans, we have the rare opportunity to become divine through spiritual practice, remembering the divine spark within us.

The love and affection Guruji has showered upon me cannot be expressed simply by saying "Thank you." We both do not expect anything from each other. I only wish for his blessings to remain with me for the rest of this lifetime and, if possible, in future lifetimes. As a token of my gratitude, I have begun writing this book in honour of my Guruji as a biography.

This book, based on the teachings of Kandhaguru Guruji, transcends categorization, addressing everything from the individual's quest for meaning to the urgent social and economic issues of our time. It is not a conventional written work but rather a collection of transcriptions from Guruji's extemporaneous talks, delivered over time during Sunday Kriya Yogam classes in various cities across Tamil Nadu and Karnataka.

Guruji's mission has been to create the conditions for the birth of a new kind of human being—the Kriya Yogi—one who remains grounded while reaching for the stars. His teachings reflect a profound vision that combines the timeless wisdom of the East with an approach to inner transformation that is suited to the demands of modern life.

Guruji's revolutionary contributions to meditation focus on practices that address the accelerated pace of contemporary life. The techniques he teaches are designed to release accumulated stress from the body and mind, making it easier to find stillness and experience a thought-free state of meditation.

This book serves as an introduction to Kriya Yogam and is intended to benefit newcomers who are stepping onto the spiritual path.

With deep blessings,
IVS Srinivas

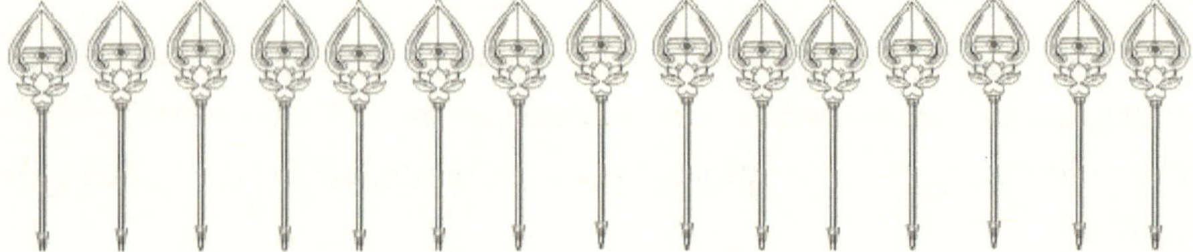

"Aligning with the Rhythm of Nature"

Embrace the rhythm of nature.

Be like the earth—grounded, nurturing, and unwavering.

Be like the tree—rooted in stillness,

yet reaching for the sky with quiet grace.

When you align yourself with the pure essence of life,

your human consciousness will blossom effortlessly,

revealing its natural beauty and Wisdom.

SRI KANDHAGURU FOUNDATION

"Aum Hreem Shree Gurubhyo Namaha"

Infinite thanks to Guruji who taught me Kriya.

Infinite thanks to Mahavatar Babaji.

Thanks to the universe.

Thanks to the five elements.

Thanks to my soul.

"This work is a task assigned to me by God.'"

Contents

Arputha Amrutham

In every step, there is a temple,
Inside everyone, there is a temple,
In that temple, there is light,
That light is God, let's go inside and see.
Love you, Shiva, love you, Shiva,
In your light, we are free,
Love you, Shiva, love you, Shiva,
In your heart, we'll always stay.
In silence deep, a sound we hear,
A gentle call that draws us near.
It speaks of love, it speaks of peace,
A quiet song that never ceases.
Love you, Shiva, love you, Shiva,
In your light, we find our way.
Love you, Shiva, love you, Shiva,
In your heart, we'll always stay.
Each breath we take is filled with you,
Your light shines bright in all we do.
Behind the world, beyond the skies,
Your endless love opens our eyes.
Love you, Shiva, love you, Shiva,
In your light, we are free,
Love you, Shiva, love you, Shiva,
In your heart, we'll always stay.

In the stillness, we are whole,
In your grace, we find our soul,
Step by step, we walk the path,
In your presence, there's no wrath.
In silence deep, a sound we hear,
A gentle call that draws us near.
It speaks of love, it speaks of peace,
A quiet song that never ceases.
Love you, Shiva, love you, Shiva,
In your light, we find our way.
Love you, Shiva, love you, Shiva,
In your heart, we'll always stay.
In every step, there is a temple,
Inside everyone, there is a temple,
In that temple, there is light,
That light is God, let's go inside and see.

Kriya Amrutham

Embracing the Divine Presence of Babaji in Everyday Life.

Working closely with God is a central goal in many spiritual paths, including Hinduism, Christianity, and other faiths. In Hinduism, particularly through the teachings of sages like Shree Yajnavalkya Maharshi, this concept involves building a profound personal relationship with the Divine, realizing that the self (Atman) and God (Brahman) are one, not separate.

In Kriya Yogam, this connection is deepened through specific techniques that enhance self-awareness and inner peace. Instead of simply seeking to meet divine beings like Mahavatar Babaji, pray to him for his blessings, that he may be with you, guide you, and teach you. Feel his presence in your heart, and meditate on him. By focusing on him in your heart, you will connect with him deeply and soulfully.

Always feel that Mahavatar Babaji is present in your home, and consider him a part of your family. Keep a seat ready for him next to you when you talk to others, while eating, during your Kriya practice, and in every activity you do. By making him a part of your daily life, you invite his divine presence into your home and heart, allowing his guidance and blessings to flow naturally through all that you do. This deep connection with Babaji fosters a constant sense of divine companionship, helping you feel his support in every moment.

Through the practice of Kriya Yogam and focused meditation, we can experience a soulful connection with the Divine, allowing us to transcend the limitations of the physical world and reach a deeper spiritual understanding.

Preface

Introduction to Kriya Yogam and Spiritual Path

Kriya Yogam stands out as a timeless guide to self-discovery and inner peace, offering a profound path for those seeking to connect with the divine. The journey begins with a simple question: Who am I? This quest leads us to explore deeper dimensions of ourselves, often igniting a transformative spark within.

This book is designed for beginners in Kriya Yogam and those drawn to the teachings of Shree Mahavatar Babaji, whose wisdom is not just spiritual doctrine but a beacon of hope for those seeking a deeper connection with themselves and the divine.

Shree Mahavatar Babaji: The Immortal Yogi

Shree Mahavatar Babaji is revered as the "immortal yogi," embodying divine love, compassion, and wisdom. His teachings on Kriya Yogam offer practical methods for personal transformation, opening a gateway to purpose, peace, and spiritual fulfillment. Through his guidance, countless seekers across generations have awakened their inner potential and experienced the divine presence within.

The Importance of a Guru in Spiritual Practice

For those beginning their spiritual journey, the path can feel overwhelming due to the vastness of knowledge. Here, a living guru plays a crucial role. A guru provides personalized guidance, helping to navigate the spiritual terrain with wisdom, patience, and protection from potential pitfalls. Just as a traveler relies on a guide in unfamiliar territory, the guru's presence ensures clarity, spiritual transformation, and steady progress.

Kriya Yogam: A Way of Life

Kriya Yogam is more than a set of techniques—it is a way of life. When practiced with sincerity and consistency, it sharpens the mind, opens the heart, and harmonizes the practitioner with the universe. This path becomes a lifelong companion, bringing peace, joy, and a deep sense of connection that transcends the ordinary. Through dedication, Kriya Yogam leads to profound inner transformation.

The Role of Religions in Connecting with the Divine

Every religion offers a unique path to connect with the Divine. Sincere devotion, regardless of faith, leads to spiritual realization. Figures like Jesus, Muhammad, Buddha, and Ramakrishna Paramahamsa have demonstrated how following a spiritual path can transcend our limits, guiding us to the Divine. While religions like Christianity, Islam, and Buddhism were founded by visionaries, Hinduism stands apart as Sanatana Dharma, an "eternal" path with no single founder.

In ancient times, Rishis, through deep meditation, channeled divine wisdom that became the Vedas. These texts explored the relationship between Brahma (the Creator) and the individual soul (Purusha), which was simplified into the Upanishads. The essence of these teachings, including the famous "Tat Tvam Asi" (You are that), was further distilled into the Bhagavad Gita. In the Gita, Krishna represents divine consciousness, and Arjuna symbolizes the individual consciousness. The Gita teaches paths of realization through Jnana Yoga, Karma Yoga, Bhakti Yoga, and Raja Yoga.

Religious Harmony and Spiritual Progress

Religions, while offering different paths, all aim to guide us toward spiritual well-being. Just as two selfless individuals step aside to allow each other to pass on a narrow path, spiritual growth involves embracing all paths to the Divine. Great souls like Jesus, Muhammad, Buddha, and Ramakrishna

Paramahamsa have shown that truth, fairness, and integrity endure across all religions. By walking our paths with dignity and fostering religious harmony, we can guide others toward the Divine.

In summary, Kriya Yogam is a profound practice that not only offers techniques for meditation and personal growth but also serves as a spiritual companion on the path to self-awareness and divine connection. It encourages consistency, patience, and humility, and it reminds us that all religions ultimately aim to guide us to the same Divine truth.

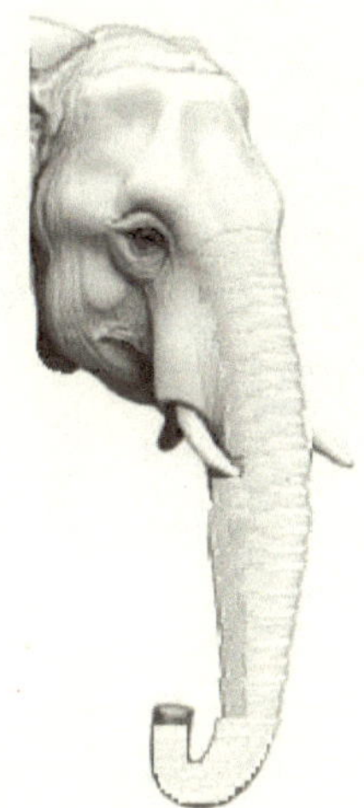

Kriya Amrutham 1

A Glimpse into the Divine Journey of Guruji

Before we embark on the chapter of Guruji's life journey, let us pause and reflect upon the deeper meaning of his path. His life is not merely a tale of personal achievement, but a beacon of divine wisdom, selfless service, and unwavering devotion to truth. It is a testament to the transformative power of humility, compassion, and spiritual strength.

Guruji's journey teaches us that true greatness lies not in worldly accolades, but in living a life of purpose, guided by love and righteousness. Each step he took was one of surrender to the divine will, showing us that the key to peace and fulfillment is found in surrendering our ego and embracing the grace of the Creator.

Though our Guru walks ahead of us, he shares in our struggles and challenges, having experienced them before. His wisdom and compassion guide us on the same spiritual path he has already traversed, helping us draw closer to divine truth.

As we read on, let us approach his story with an open heart, allowing his words and actions to inspire us to live more consciously, with reverence and respect for all that is sacred in this world. May his life lead us towards the path of light, leading us closer to the divine truth.

SUMMA IRU SUGAMAI IRU
Endrum Anandhamai iru

Chapter 1

Shree Khandhaguru Guruji's Life Journey

"My journey into the spiritual path began when I was just a boy of 12 years. It was my beloved grandfather, Sri Kandhaguru, who first introduced me to the ancient wisdom of Kriya Yogam. I was drawn to its depth even at that tender age, though I did not yet fully grasp its transformative power. Little did I know then that this introduction would lay the foundation for the journey of self-discovery and spiritual awakening that would define my life.

Years later, at the age of 32, I felt an unshakable calling within my heart—a yearning that could not be ignored. I left my village behind and embarked on a journey to the sacred Amarnath. Known for its divine energy and spiritual significance, this holy site drew seekers from all walks of life. There, amidst the serene mountains and the company of ascetics and monks, my destiny unfolded. It was there that I met my true Master—Sri Mouna Siddhar, a direct disciple of the great Mahavatar Babaji Maharaj himself.

Sri Mouna Siddhar saw within me a readiness to tread the sacred path of Kriya Yogam. With his infinite grace, he accepted me as his disciple. For 48 days, I remained under his close guidance, learning the profound techniques of Kriya Yogam. Those days were a blessing beyond measure, as they gave me not only the sacred knowledge but also the strength to walk the path of self-realization. It was during this time that I received the initiation into Kriya Yogam—a moment that forever changed the course of my life.

Upon my return, I immersed myself completely in the practice of Kriya Yogam. I applied its techniques diligently, navigating the ups and downs of life with newfound clarity and peace. Over the next eight years, my practice deepened, and I experienced a profound transformation. I began to understand how to free myself from the struggles, distractions, and burdens of the material world.

In 2019, after years of intense practice and spiritual growth, I was guided to establish the Sri Kandhaguru Foundation in Bhavani, Erode District, Tamil Nadu. The purpose of this Foundation was clear—to share the timeless teachings of Kriya Yogam with all who sought spiritual growth and inner peace. I wanted to create a space where seekers could learn and practice these techniques under direct guidance, as I once had.

Since then, the work of the Foundation has grown in ways I could not have imagined. Thousands of seekers from Tamil Nadu and beyond have come to learn Kriya Yogam. To date, I have been blessed to initiate over 15,342 students into this sacred practice. Watching them transform their lives through the teachings of Kriya Yogam brings me immense joy and fulfillment.

My mission is simple yet profound—to guide each seeker to discover the divinity within themselves. Through the Sri Kandhaguru Foundation, I continue to serve this purpose, offering a path to inner peace, transformation, and self-realization. This journey is not mine alone; it is a shared journey, and I walk it alongside all those who seek the light within."

With blessings and gratitude,

Kandhaguru Guruji

Kriya Amrutham 2

Shree Mahavatar Babaji

1. Eternal and Immortal Nature

Babaji is believed to possess a deathless body that remains ever-youthful, transcending time and space. His immortality symbolizes a life fully merged with divine consciousness.

2. Supreme Compassion

He radiates boundless love and compassion, tirelessly guiding humanity toward spiritual liberation without expecting anything in return.

3. Complete Detachment

Babaji is untouched by material desires or worldly attachments, representing the ultimate ideal of renunciation.

4. Omniscience

Babaji's consciousness is said to encompass all realms, granting him profound insight into the needs of each soul and the cosmic plan.

5. Spiritual Authority

As the reviver of Kriya Yogam, Babaji plays the role of a spiritual architect, offering humanity a powerful tool for enlightenment while orchestrating the work of many saints and avatars.

6. Master of Siddhis (Supernatural Powers)

He is known to wield mastery over siddhis, such as teleportation, materialization, and control over nature, yet he uses them solely for divine purposes.

7. Humility and Simplicity

Despite his cosmic stature, Babaji operates humbly, often remaining unseen, working silently to uplift humanity.

Chapter 2

Mahavatar Babaji

The Immortal Presence of Mahavatar Babaji

Mahavatar Babaji, whose name translates to "Great Avatar Dear Father," is a figure of legend, revered as an immortal yogi and spiritual master. His existence, believed to span centuries, is intertwined with the sacred Himalayas, where he is thought to have lived since the early centuries of the Common Era. Babaji is credited with reviving Kriya Yogam, a transformative spiritual practice that harmonizes breath control, meditation, and the awakening of kundalini energy—leading one to self-realization and divine connection.

Babaji's story begins in 203 A.D. in Tamil Nadu, India, where he was born as Nagaraj, meaning "serpent king." This name symbolized his deep connection with kundalini energy, the latent spiritual power within all of us. His birth on November 30th, during the Kartikai Deepam Festival, under the Rohini star, marked the arrival of a spiritual luminary destined to guide humanity. His family, the Nambudri Brahmins, were temple priests, and it was here that young Nagaraj first encountered the sacred teachings of his culture.

At the tender age of five, Nagaraj's life took a dramatic turn when he was kidnapped and later rescued by a wealthy merchant in what is now Calcutta. During his journey, he joined wandering monks, thirsting for deeper spiritual knowledge. This led him to Sri Lanka at age eleven, where he sought the guidance of Bhogarnathar, a disciple of the renowned Siddha master Agastyar. Under their tutelage, Nagaraj delved into advanced yogic practices, including meditation and the technique of Kriya Kundalini Pranayama, a powerful breathwork practice that awakens the dormant spiritual energy within.

By age fifteen, Nagaraj retreated into the Himalayas, fully surrendering to the Divine. In this sacred solitude, he achieved mastery over his body and mind, becoming a "siddha"—a perfected being free from disease, aging, and death. His transformation was so profound that he is said to have transcended the physical limitations of the human body, remaining in a youthful form even as centuries passed. Babaji, in his divine compassion, chose to share the transformative power of Kriya Yogam with the world.

In 1861, Babaji appeared to the yogi Lahiri Mahasaya and initiated him into Kriya Yogam, thus igniting a lineage of spiritual teachers that would include revered figures like Sri Yukteswar and Paramahansa Yogananda. Babaji's disciples believe he has transcended physical death, remaining alive in the Himalayas for over 2,000 years, manifesting in a youthful form of around 16 to 20 years old. His continuous presence among us, though subtle and often unseen, offers spiritual guidance to those who are ready to receive it.

In the Siddha tradition, Babaji is not just a spiritual master but a being who has gained control over the five elements—fire, water, air, earth, and space—demonstrating extraordinary yogic powers. These include the ability to sit in fire without harm, merge with water, fly through the air, and materialize at will. These mystical abilities, described in the Yogam Sutras of Patanjali, are the fruits of deep, focused meditation and the practice of *samyama*—a state of deep concentration, meditation, and superconsciousness. Babaji's siddhis serve as a reminder of the infinite possibilities available to those who attain mastery over their inner nature.

Though Babaji remains hidden from the physical world, he continues to guide select disciples through subtle visions and divine interventions. His teachings on Kriya Yogam are not just about physical practices—they are a gateway to enlightenment, a path to self-realization.

Through his sacred guidance, countless individuals have awakened to the divine presence within themselves, experiencing the peace, joy, and clarity that come from a life aligned with higher spiritual principles.

Over the centuries, Babaji has appeared to saints, sages, and spiritual reformers, including the great Adi Shankaracharya and the saint Kabir, offering support and blessings on their journeys.

His mission is clear: to elevate human consciousness, bring divine light into the world, and help each person realize their highest spiritual potential. Even today, Babaji's influence is believed to subtly guide humanity toward a greater understanding of our true nature, embodying universal love and wisdom for all who seek enlightenment.

For those who wish to connect more deeply with Babaji, there are several ways to invite his presence into your life:

1. **Visit His Cave in Ranikhet, Uttarakhand**: Babaji once meditated in this cave, and it is said to hold a special spiritual energy. Visitors often feel his presence, especially those sensitive to energy.
2. **Chant His Mantras**: The mantra "Om Kriya Babaji Namah Aum" is a sacred invocation to Babaji. Reciting this mantra with devotion can bring you closer to his divine presence, helping you experience inner transformation and spiritual progress. Another powerful mantra is " Aum Hreem Shree Gurubhyo Namaha " It is particularly effective during times of difficulty, bringing relief and connection with Babaji's energy.

3. **Practice Kriya Yogam**: Engaging in the sincere practice of Kriya Yogam is one of the most powerful ways to draw Babaji's attention. Through Kriya, Babaji supports those who are truly seeking God, guiding their spiritual journey in unique and deeply personal ways.

Through these practices, Babaji's boundless compassion and divine wisdom are available to all who seek them. May we all connect with this immortal being, and in doing so, come closer to understanding our true nature and purpose in this life.

Advanced Information on Mahavatar Babaji's Traits

1. Immortal Consciousness:

Babaji exists in a state of **nirvikalpa samadhi**, the highest state of consciousness where the individual self merges with universal oneness. This enables him to maintain his physical body indefinitely while remaining rooted in divine awareness. His immortality reflects the ideal of overcoming the cycle of birth and death, as taught in yogic scriptures.

2. Role as a Spiritual Catalyst

Babaji's work is not limited to a specific time or place. He guides and inspires spiritual movements globally, appearing to seekers and masters across cultures when they are ready for higher teachings. His influence extends beyond individuals to shaping the evolution of human consciousness as a whole.

3. Mastery over Maya (Illusion)

Babaji transcends the dualities of creation—pleasure and pain, life and death, good and evil. His mastery over maya signifies perfect alignment with **Ishwara shakti**, the divine will. He can manifest forms or events purely to assist aspirants on their spiritual journey.

4. Dynamic Silence

Though often silent and elusive, Babaji's silence is not passive; it is a **dynamic force** that transforms the consciousness of those who meditate on him or his teachings. His presence can ignite inner spiritual transformation without direct communication.

5. Universal Relevance

Babaji's teachings and methods, especially Kriya Yogam, are timeless and transcend religious boundaries. His approach emphasizes **self-realization**, enabling aspirants to connect with the divine light within themselves, which he perceives as the true essence of all beings.

6. Infinite Patience

Babaji's work spans eons, patiently guiding humanity toward a golden age of enlightenment. He allows seekers to grow at their own pace, never forcing transformation, embodying divine patience.

Mahavatar Babaji is not just a personality but a manifestation of divine principles in human form, embodying both the ideal yogi and the cosmic guru. Through his silent, compassionate guidance, he continues to be a beacon of light for sincere spiritual seekers.

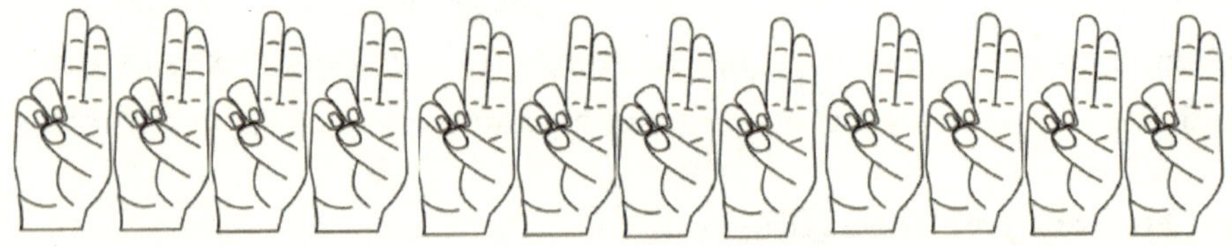

Prana Mudra

Kriya Amrutham 3

Siddhargal: Masters of Transcendence

The Siddhargal, often revered as enlightened beings, are the custodians of divine knowledge and the mystical sciences of Yoga, Tantra, and alchemy. Rooted in the Tamil Siddha tradition, these ancient sages mastered the intricate pathways of the body, mind, and soul, unlocking the secrets of immortality and divine consciousness.

In the realm of Kriya Yogam, Siddhargal play a pivotal role. Their advanced techniques of pranayama and meditation offer direct insights into the realms of higher awareness. The Siddhargal emphasized that the human body is a microcosm of the universe—through the activation of energy centers (chakras) and nadis (energy pathways), one can transcend the boundaries of time and space.

Advanced Insights

1. *Siddha Kriyas: The Siddhargal developed specific kriyas that harmonize the physical and astral bodies, enabling practitioners to experience "Kayakalpa," a state of rejuvenation and spiritual transformation. These kriyas serve as a bridge between mundane existence and higher states of samadhi.*
2. *The Science of Light and Sound: Siddhargal viewed the cosmos as an interplay of sound (Nada) and light (Bindu). They revealed mantras and bija sounds to resonate with these cosmic frequencies, which are integral to advanced Kriya practices.*

3. *Subtle Elements Mastery: The Siddhargal taught that mastering the five subtle elements—earth, water, fire, air, and ether—leads to siddhis (spiritual powers). However, they warned against the misuse of these powers, emphasizing their purpose in self-realization and universal service.*
4. *Immortal Wisdom: Legends narrate that some Siddhargal achieved an imperishable state through their sadhana. Mahavatar Babaji himself is often linked to this tradition, embodying their eternal guidance and grace.*

This chapter illuminates the profound contribution of Siddhargal to Kriya Yogam, inspiring readers to delve deeper into their practices and connect with this timeless lineage.

Chapter 3

Siddhargal

Origins of the Siddhars and Kriya Yogam

Siddhar teachings and Kriya Yogam both offer transformative practices that promote physical health, spiritual growth, and inner mastery. With techniques centered around breath control, meditation, and energy alignment, Kriya Yogam reflects Siddhar wisdom, presenting a holistic approach to well-being and spiritual enlightenment. These timeless teachings from the Siddhars, preserved and passed through Kriya Yogam, remain invaluable for those seeking inner healing and divine connection.

1. Introduction to Siddhars and Kriya Yogam

The Siddhars were ancient mystics primarily from Tamil Nadu in South India, known for their mastery in yoga, alchemy, medicine, and spirituality. The term "Siddhar" derives from *siddhi*, meaning "perfection" or "attainment." Siddhars aimed to achieve both physical and spiritual mastery, aspiring toward divine wisdom and profound inner transformation.

Their teachings are rooted in Tamil Shaiva Siddhanta philosophy, which emphasizes liberation (*moksha*) and union with the Divine. Many of their teachings, preserved in sacred texts like *Thirumandiram* by Siddhar Thirumular, delve into advanced Yogam practices and alchemical knowledge.

Kriya Yogam, while distinct, shares its foundation with these ancient practices. The modern Kriya Yogam tradition was reintroduced in the 19th century by Mahavatar Babaji, a revered immortal yogi often linked to the Siddhar lineage. Babaji's teachings were passed down through Lahiri Mahasaya and later popularized by Paramahansa Yogananda, bringing Kriya Yogam to a global audience as a powerful path to spiritual growth and inner peace.

2. Key Teachings of the Siddhars

The Siddhars combined profound spiritual wisdom with practical knowledge to foster holistic personal growth. Their core teachings include:

a) Inner Alchemy

Siddhars believed the body was a vessel for divine energy, requiring purification to reach higher spiritual states. Through yogic practices, they taught that one could transform the mind and body, preparing for spiritual awakening.

b) Supernatural Powers (Ashta Siddhis)

Siddhars described eight supernatural abilities (*ashta siddhis*)—such as invisibility and levitation—achieved through dedicated practice. They cautioned that these powers, while remarkable, should not distract from the ultimate goal of liberation.

c) Siddha Medicine

Siddhars pioneered Siddha medicine, a system balancing the body's energies (*vata*, *pitta*, and *kapha*) using herbs and minerals. They believed physical health was essential for spiritual progress, as bodily imbalances could hinder spiritual growth.

d) Kundalini Awakening and Divine Union

Siddhars emphasized the awakening of Kundalini Shakti, the spiritual energy at the spine's base. This awakening, an alchemical process, allows practitioners to achieve union with Shiva, or pure consciousness.

e) Immortality and Transcendence

Some Siddhars, including Mahavatar Babaji, are believed to have attained immortality, transcending physical limitations through intense yogic practices. Liberation from the cycle of birth and death was considered their ultimate goal.

3. Kriya Yogam's Connection with Siddhar Teachings

Though the Siddhars did not specifically refer to "Kriya Yogam," their practices align closely with its principles. Kriya Yogam, as revived by Babaji, integrates pranayama (breath control), meditation, and energy regulation to purify the mind and body, awaken Kundalini, and attain spiritual liberation.

a) Pranayama (Breath Control)

Both Siddhar practices and Kriya Yogam emphasize breath control. In Kriya Yogam, pranayama channels energy along the spine, cleansing energy pathways (*nadis*). Siddhars viewed pranayama as essential for balancing body and mind, preparing practitioners for deep meditation.

b) Energy Centers and Kundalini

Kriya Yogam's focus on channeling energy through the spine mirrors the Siddhars' teachings on Kundalini Shakti. Moving energy through chakras aligns with the Siddhar aim of merging Shiva (consciousness) and Shakti (energy).

c) Meditation and Inner Silence

Kriya Yogam encourages deep meditation to transcend the ego and experience divine union. Similarly, Siddhars viewed meditation as a path to *turiya*, a state beyond ordinary consciousness, to achieve oneness with the Divine.

d) Purification and Inner Alchemy

The purification practices in Kriya Yogam resonate with the Siddhar concept of inner alchemy. Siddhars believed purification was essential for attaining higher states of awareness and advancing spiritually.

e) Liberation and Self-Realization

Liberation (*moksha*) was the Siddhars' ultimate goal, and Kriya Yogam similarly aims to help practitioners transcend the ego and realize their divine nature, freeing them from the cycle of rebirth.

4. Healing Benefits of Kriya Yogam According to Siddhar Tradition

The Siddhars believed Kriya-like practices could foster holistic health, addressing numerous ailments by balancing bodily energies.

Key health benefits include:

- **Strengthening the Respiratory System:** Kriya Yogam's pranayama practices improve lung capacity and oxygenation, benefiting respiratory health.
- **Mental Health Support:** Kriya Yogam calms the mind, alleviating stress-related conditions like anxiety and depression.
- **Enhanced Digestion:** These practices support digestive health, aiding in conditions like indigestion.
- **Improved Circulation and Cardiovascular Health:** Kriya Yogam's stress-reducing effects help stabilize blood pressure and heart health.
- **Nervous System Benefits:** Meditation and pranayama strengthen the nervous system, fostering mental clarity and resilience.
- **Boosted Immunity:** Balanced prana (life force) strengthens immunity, helping prevent infections and chronic illnesses.

5. Siddhar Wisdom and Unique Beliefs Related to Kriya Yogam

The Siddhars held unique beliefs about spiritual growth, longevity, and transformation, which resonate with Kriya Yogam practices.

a) Mastery over the Five Elements

Siddhars taught that Kriya Yogam helps balance the five elements (earth, water, fire, air, and ether) within the body, fostering resilience against illness and environmental stress.

b) Reverse Aging

They believed that yogic practices could slow or reverse aging by enhancing cellular vitality.

c) The Secret Fire of Immortality

The Siddhars spoke of an internal *vasi* or secret fire that could be kindled to purify karma and prolong life.

d) Balancing Solar and Lunar Energies

Kriya Yogam's breath work balances the body's solar (heating) and lunar (cooling) energies, promoting physical and mental stability.

e) Direct Cleansing of Karma

Some Siddhar teachings suggest that Kriya Yogam purifies karmic residue, a vital step toward inner peace and physical health.

f) Experiencing Divine Sound and Light

Advanced Kriya practitioners often hear divine sounds and see inner light, indicating progress and alignment with cosmic energy.

g) Connection with Divine Beings

Siddhars believed that advanced practitioners of Kriya Yogam could connect with higher spiritual beings, receiving insight and guidance.

h) Restoring Vitality and Strength

Siddhars held that Kriya practices could restore vitality and counter chronic fatigue by absorbing Prana, or life force.

i) Spiritual Ladder to Higher Consciousness

The Siddhars described Yogam as a "spiritual ladder," with Kriya Yogam providing a structured path from body consciousness to cosmic consciousness, offering insights at each stage.

Through Kriya Yogam and Siddhar teachings, practitioners embark on a journey of inner healing, self-mastery, and spiritual liberation. These paths remain relevant today, providing seekers with a step-by-step approach to experiencing divine union and a life aligned with the wisdom of the Siddhars.

Kriya Amrutham 4

A Journey to Inner Light

"Go Inside and See" invites readers to embark on a transformative inward journey to discover the divine light within themselves. This light, often referred to as the essence of pure consciousness, is the source of truth, wisdom, and joy.

In Kriya Yogam, going inward is more than a practice—it is a revelation of our highest potential. By quieting the mind and deepening our awareness, we connect with the core of our being, where divine energy resides. This inner light is not bound by time or circumstance; it is eternal and universal, present in every individual.

Through disciplined practice and self-inquiry, the barriers of ego, fear, and ignorance dissolve, allowing the light within to shine forth. This awakening is a reminder of the rare and precious opportunity human life offers: the ability to transcend limitations and experience unity with the Divine.

The chapter encourages readers to make this inner exploration a priority at least once in their lifetime. It is a call to awaken the spiritual force within, bringing clarity, balance, and a deeper connection to life's true purpose.

Chapter 4

Go inside and see

There is light in every one.
Try to go inside and look for it at least once in a life time.

Beautiful words! Yes, there is a divine light within each of us, a light of consciousness, truth, and wisdom. The journey inward, to discover and connect with this inner light, is a fundamental aspect of spiritual practices like Kriya Yogam. This light is often referred to as the Atman or the true self, beyond the mind and ego, radiating with pure awareness and love.

When we go within, through practices like meditation and self-inquiry, we begin to access this light. The process is not always immediate, but with dedication, focus, and the guidance of a true teacher, one can experience the quiet but powerful presence of this divine energy. This is what many great spiritual traditions refer to as enlightenment, or the realization of our oneness with the Divine.

Your reminder to look inward at least once in a lifetime is a call to spiritual awakening. It is through inner exploration that we uncover the deepest truths of existence, recognizing that the divine light we seek is already within us.

Often, we live life without a clear understanding of its purpose, tangled in unnecessary thoughts and confusion. The human body, however, is a marvelous mechanism, and humans hold a special place among all life on

Earth, sharing a spark of the divine. Within each of us lies a unique inner science known as *Ghaanam* (knowledge or wisdom). When this *Ghaanam* begins to work within, it reveals hidden truths that empower us to master life.

To activate this inner wisdom, practicing Kriya Yogam can help. This practice initiates a journey inward, unlocking the secrets needed to achieve greater understanding and success in life.

Unlike animals, human beings have the ability and the opportunity to become divine through worship and spiritual practice. Human birth is rare and precious (*"Aridu Aridu Manidaraay Pirathal Aridu"*), granting us a unique chance to remember and honor the divine within. Worship in temples and at home serves as a reminder, yet the true divine spark (*Sudar Oli*) is inside each of us.

For any work or business, *Ghaanam* is essential. To move out of poverty and experience prosperity, we need to nurture the light within us (*Arul Oli*) to dispel inner darkness (*Irul Oli*). By bringing this light into ourselves—gradually and consistently—we can remove obstacles and walk the path of spirituality.

The wisdom from Tamil literature encourages us to cherish this human life, to seek truth, and to grow spiritually. It is an invitation to make the most of our unique human journey by discovering the divine potential within.

God made the senses turn outwards,
man therefore looks outwards,
not into himself.
But occaionally a daring soul,
desiring immortality,
has looked back and found himself.

The Upanishads

ABOUT KRIYA YOGAM

Ardhanarishvara represents the harmonious fusion of masculine and feminine energies, embodied by Shiva and Parvati. In this depiction, Shiva occupies the right side, symbolizing the Surya Nadi or Pingala Nadi, associated with solar energy, action, and dynamic force. Parvati is on the left side, representing the Chandra Nadi or Ida Nadi, embodying lunar energy, intuition, and calming qualities.

At the center of their union, a trishul (trident) is positioned along the midline just below their faces. This trishul is not merely a weapon; it holds profound symbolic significance, representing the three primary nadis (energy channels) in the subtle body: Ida, Pingala, and Sushumna. The two outer prongs of the trishul correspond to the Ida and Pingala nadis, which spiral around the central Sushumna nadi, converging at key points along the spine.

Sushumna, the central channel symbolized by the middle prong of the trishul, is the path to spiritual awakening. It is only through balance between the Ida and Pingala, the lunar and solar energies, that the kundalini energy can rise through Sushumna, leading to spiritual enlightenment. Thus, Ardhanarishvara symbolizes not only the balance of masculine and feminine aspects within every being but also the path to spiritual wholeness through the alignment of inner energies. This union of power and unity in Ardhanarishvara serves as a powerful reminder of the interconnectedness of duality in the universe and within ourselves.

Kriya Amrutham 5

What You Gain from Learning Kriya Yogam at Kandhaguru Foundation

About This Class:

Shiva Kriya Yogam (Level 1) is a powerful spiritual practice that blends yoga, meditation, and breath control to awaken your inner self, bring peace, and help you grow spiritually. This ancient practice is inspired by the teachings of Lord Shiva, who represents transformation and ultimate truth. In this class, you'll learn how to release negative thoughts (karma) and find a deeper connection with your true self.

What You'll Learn:

- How to practice Shiva Kriya Yogam
- Techniques to control your thoughts
- Meditation practices for inner peace and focus
- How to let go of negative thoughts (karma)

Benefits:

- A healthy body and calm mind
- Inner peace and happiness
- Improved overall health and well-being
- Boosted self-confidence

- Healing of physical and mental ailments with regular practice
- A balanced and healthy lifestyle
- Enhanced career opportunities
- Personal growth and development
- Better focus and memory for students
- Reduced stress and improved performance in exams
- Greater ability to handle life's challenges and find solutions

This course is perfect for beginners who want to improve their health, mind, and life through the teachings of Kriya Yogam.

Chapter 5

Introduction to Kriya Yogam

Kriya Yogam is a profound spiritual practice designed to accelerate inner transformation and elevate consciousness. Rooted in ancient wisdom, Kriya Yogam harmonizes breath, energy, and awareness, creating a pathway to inner stillness. This stillness brings the mind to a place of peace, free from distractions and sensory perceptions. With regular practice, it calms the heart, lungs, and nervous system, paving the way for deeper self-awareness.

Often, without understanding our true essence, we become caught in endless thoughts and confusion. The human body, however, is a remarkable creation with unique potential for divine experience.

Embedded within us is an inner science called *Ghaanam*—knowledge or wisdom. When awakened, this inner wisdom reveals life's hidden secrets, guiding us toward mastery and profound fulfillment. Kriya Yogam begins this awakening, bringing forth the insights needed to understand and master life on a deeper level.

Life is more than the physical cycle of birth, growth, reproduction, and death. Human existence is a rare opportunity to explore higher awareness, enabling us to reach extraordinary states of understanding and liberation.

Within each of us lies an eternal essence, the core of our being, which expresses itself in various ways: enlightenment, self-realization, kundalini awakening, the opening of the third eye, and more. The journey to understand this eternal nature is the path that leads beyond the cycles of birth and death.

This wisdom has been preserved and shared by great beings like Siddhas, sages, and enlightened masters, who passed down their sacred knowledge through devoted disciples. Among the paths to enlightenment,

VasiYogam is a unique and powerful method, emphasized by the Yogic Insights Foundation under the guidance of Brahmashree Thavaththiru Thiruchitrambala Swamigal. Kriya Yogam offers a similar transformative approach, bringing peace, joy, and a deep sense of harmony within and with the world.

Core Principles of Kriya Yogam

Kriya Yogam works by regulating the breath, which is closely linked with *Prana* (life energy). Rhythmic breathing aligns the breath with Prana, guiding energy along the spine, particularly through the Ida, Pingala, and Sushumna channels. As Prana flows upward, the practitioner's awareness moves from the physical to the divine.

Regular, dedicated practice creates significant physical, mental, and spiritual benefits. Below are the core aspects of Kriya Yogam:

1. **Breath Control and Prana:** Controlling the breath is central to Kriya Yogam, as it directs Prana to clear mental and emotional blockages. Techniques like pranayama balance the Ida (left), Pingala (right), and Sushumna (central) channels along the spine, harmonizing mind and body.
2. **Awakening Consciousness:** By guiding Prana through the chakras, Kriya Yogam opens dormant spiritual centers along the spine, including the Sahasrara chakra at the crown, associated with higher awareness and divine connection.
3. **Energy Redirection:** Through specific techniques, Kriya Yogam channels energy from the Mooladhara (root chakra) upwards, supporting spiritual growth and deep inner peace.
4. **The Role of the Guru:** A Guru is essential in Kriya Yogam, providing guidance, initiation, and protection. This relationship ensures that practitioners progress safely and effectively along their spiritual path.

5. **Meditation:** Meditation is a vital part of Kriya Yogam, helping practitioners reach a state of pure awareness. Techniques like Aum chanting and breath focus quiet the mind and deepen meditation, promoting higher consciousness.
6. **Consistency of Practice:** Practicing daily for 45-60 minutes improves mental clarity, emotional balance, and spiritual progress. Regular practice breaks negative patterns and nurtures lasting peace.
7. **Advanced Practices and Spiritual Development:** As one progresses, refined techniques are introduced to increase energy flow and access higher awareness. These advanced practices are typically taught through initiation by a qualified teacher.

Scientific Benefits of Kriya Yogam

Scientific research shows that Yogam practices like Kriya Yogam can enhance mental and physical health. Studies indicate that Kriya Yogam promotes brain plasticity, enhances memory, sharpens focus, and improves emotional stability. Regular practice stimulates the brain areas linked to higher cognitive functions, including memory, focus, and mental clarity.

In Conclusion

Kriya Yogam offers a comprehensive path to self-realization and inner peace. Through dedication and practice, it accelerates spiritual growth, fosters mental clarity, and enhances awareness, making it an invaluable tool for those seeking higher consciousness and fulfillment.

Kriya Amrutham 6

"Having trouble with

low Memory retention and

exam performance?

If your attendance is

perfect but your

understanding is only

halfway there,

the solution is simple,

practice Kriya Yogam.

It helps improve Memory

retention and boosts

your results."

Chapter 6

Elegibility to do Kriya

The Call and Commitment of Kriya Yogam

When life is packed with responsibilities—work, family, personal goals—the idea of adding something as seemingly demanding as a daily hour of Kriya Yogam can feel daunting. You might wonder, *What does this practice offer me?* Or, *How will Kriya Yogam truly benefit my life, given all my other obligations?*

Kriya Yogam offers something profound: a doorway into a clearer, calmer, and more vibrant version of yourself. It provides not only the means to handle the demands of life but to find fulfillment beyond them, in a deeper space of peace and self-discovery. For anyone feeling the inner call, Kriya Yogam meets you where you are and invites you on a transformative journey. But it does ask for sincerity, commitment, and, most importantly, the willingness to walk this path with devotion.

What It Takes to Begin

Kriya Yogam is not an exclusive practice, but there are qualities that help make the journey fruitful. Here's what it requires:

1. **Sincerity and Dedication**: This isn't a casual practice. It's a commitment to a transformative journey, where regularity, patience, and a true interest in spiritual growth bring the deepest benefits. If approached with dedication, Kriya becomes a steady companion in your growth.
2. **Consistency and Discipline**: Practicing Kriya daily, ideally for about an hour, is essential. Consistency builds the strength and focus that sustain progress, helping you reach depths of awareness that sporadic practice cannot.

3. **An Open and Receptive Mind**: A willingness to let go of rigid beliefs opens you to the insights that Kriya can reveal. With an open mind, the inner shifts brought on by the practice become easier to embrace.
4. **Physical and Mental Stability**: Good physical and mental health make practicing Kriya Yogam easier. Since Kriya involves controlled breathing and meditation, health issues can make it more challenging. However, even with some imperfections, a stable state of mind and body can support the inner journey Kriya Yogam offers.
5. **Humility and Respect for the Tradition**: Kriya Yogam is part of a long lineage, and respect for this tradition and the guidance of a teacher adds to the depth of the practice. Humility brings sincerity and reverence, fostering a profound connection with the teachings.
6. **Curiosity and Patience for Inner Growth**: Kriya's benefits may not be instantly visible. Growth unfolds gradually, so a patient and curious heart supports you during periods where the effects may feel subtle.

The Calling for Kriya Yogam

Kriya Yogam often calls to those who feel there is more to life than meets the eye. These seekers are drawn not by fleeting goals but by a soul-deep urge to explore life's mysteries and discover their true nature. This yearning sustains the seeker, guiding them through the patience and dedication that Kriya requires. It is a journey of quiet perseverance rather than a quest for quick fixes.

The Subtle Power of Kriya Yogam

Unlike practices that seek to bring swift changes or sensory gratification, Kriya Yogam gradually transforms your inner landscape. It's not about accumulating powers or achieving supernatural feats but rather cultivating peace, wisdom, and a lasting sense of inner freedom. The deeper you go, the more centered and compassionate you become—less drawn to fleeting outcomes and more attuned to the timeless truths within.

Through the Kriya journey, you find a way to manage your emotions and life experiences with steadiness. Kriya gently brings suppressed feelings, memories, and old fears to the surface, allowing you to face and release them. It's a process of clearing emotional and mental layers, helping you experience your emotions as passing waves rather than getting caught in them.

Living with Ethical Balance

Kriya amplifies qualities that already exist within, so living a life grounded in honesty, kindness, and moderation helps create a strong foundation for practice. These qualities support Kriya's work on the mind and spirit, grounding you with clarity and humility. Thcy align with the yogic principle of *sthitaprajna*, a steady wisdom unshaken by life's highs and lows, as described in the *Bhagavad Gita.*

Preparation of Body and Breath

Kriya works closely with *prana*, the life force. A relatively healthy body helps the practice flourish. Asanas (Yogam postures) and pranayama (breathing exercises) keep the body flexible and the mind focused. The breath, in particular, acts as a bridge, guiding the mind from its usual restless state into profound stillness. This inner control lays a foundation for higher awareness.

The Importance of a Teacher

Kriya Yogam is traditionally taught by a guru or qualified teacher—someone who has walked this path and understands its nuances. The teacher becomes a guide, helping you move forward at a safe and steady pace, refining your practice over time. This relationship, based on mutual respect, infuses Kriya with the wisdom of the lineage, creating a sacred connection between teacher and student.

The Subtle, Transformative Journey

Kriya Yogam suits those ready for steady, committed practice. Results are subtle yet powerful, arising quietly over time. With patience and dedication, insights bloom and spiritual growth unfolds naturally. Practitioners come to live with a quiet faith, no longer driven by the desire for extraordinary experiences but by a peace that arises from the depths of regular practice.

Science and Structure in Kriya Yogam

Kriya Yogam aligns with the science of the body's energy channels—Ida, Pingala, and Sushumna. Most daily activities only require the energy flowing through Ida and Pingala. However, Kriya focuses on cleansing and opening the Sushumna, the central energy channel. This channel, when unblocked, enables the flow of higher consciousness and facilitates spiritual awakening.

Practices like Mouna Vratha (the vow of silence) are also part of Kriya Yogam's approach, helping conserve energy by minimizing speech and focusing the mind. Both external and internal silence help center the mind and channel energy inward.

Purifying Body, Mind, and Heart

Spiritual clarity begins with a "clean-up" of the body and mind. The *Bhagavad Gita* recommends moderation in food, sleep, and other habits to avoid the extremes that disrupt balance. Regular physical purification, like asanas, and moderate exercise clear the body's energy channels, while pranayama regulates and uplifts the breath. A balanced diet and avoiding substances that lower mental and spiritual energy are also beneficial.

As the body becomes purified, attention shifts to clearing the mind. Meditation gradually disciplines and stills the mind, centering it on the path of Kriya.

The Discipline of Daily Practice

Regular practice forms the backbone of Kriya Yogam. Skipping a day might not have drastic effects, but the accumulation of energy and balance from consistent practice becomes noticeable over time. An early morning practice in the stillness of *Brahma Muhurta* (around 3:20 a.m. to 4:20 a.m.) being most beneficial.

The Seven Steps to Kriya Yogam

Kriya follows a progressive series of seven steps:

- **Step 1:** Meditation practices
- **Step 2:** Energy control and mental focus
- **Step 3:** Devotion and opening the heart
- **Step 4:** Connection with the guru
- **Step 5:** The Aum technique for expanded awareness
- **Step 6:** Preparation for the deeper stages of Kriya
- **Step 7:** Initiation into Kriya proper

These steps encourage a holistic journey, moving from grounding meditation to higher spiritual awakenings.

In the end, Kriya Yogam invites you to quiet the mind, open the heart, and live in harmony with your true self. With time, practice, and sincere commitment, you'll discover a peace that's beyond words—one that resides within and guides you throughout life's journey.Bottom of Form

These guidelines emphasize the importance of purity, discipline, and humility on the spiritual path, offering practical steps for daily life and inner growth. Here's a breakdown of the key teachings and how they relate to a spiritual practice like Kriya Yogam:

1. **Guru as God:** Recognize and respect the Guru as a divine guide, honouring their teachings with faith and obedience. The Guru is seen as a living conduit of divine wisdom, and following their guidance fully can help one grow spiritually.

2. **Generosity with God's Presence;** Be generous in sharing spiritual insight and love with others, knowing that God is always present with you. This attitude cultivates a mind-set of abundance, faith, and connection.

3. **Speak Sweetly and Politely:** Kindness in speech spreads peace, aligns with inner calm, and reflects spiritual maturity. Practicing sweet speech allows the energy of your words to uplift rather than harm others.

4. **Jealousy and Humility:** Jealousy clouds the mind and creates disturbances in the soul's peace. Humility and self-contentment foster an open, grateful, and receptive heart.

5. **Practice Silence and Restraint:** Silence and reduced speech help conserve energy and focus the mind, which is essential in meditative practices. Silence is seen as a pathway to deeper wisdom and self-reflection.

6. **Avoid Unnecessary Reactions:** Non-reactivity to external events builds inner strength and detachment, reducing the "ego's" tendency to assert itself and promoting a calm and balanced response.

7. **Ego Awareness:** Ego, when unchecked, can lead to pride and defensiveness. Regular ego-checks promote humility, which is essential for spiritual growth.

8. **Physical and Mental Cleanliness:** Cleanliness in body, thoughts, and environment is considered vital for clarity and spiritual purity. This includes refraining from harmful influences, such as substances or toxic thoughts, to maintain a high vibrational state.

9. **Control of Anger and Temper:** Anger can dismantle the progress made through Kriya, as it scatters the energy cultivated in practice. Developing patience and understanding leads to emotional stability.

10. **Dietary Discipline:** Avoiding intoxicants and non-vegetarian foods aligns with sattvic (pure) qualities, which support clear thinking, stable emotions, and a lighter, more receptive energy body.

11. **Conduct:** Aligning actions with values that honor oneself, family, and God helps to prevent karmic burdens and supports a path of integrity and self-respect.

These practices cultivate a life of clarity, calmness, and connection, allowing the effects of Kriya Yogam to deepen and harmonize with daily life. They aim to make one a vessel for peace and light in the world.

Kriya Amrutham 7

The Guru's Embrace

Within you lies a power so bright,
A spark that can reach an endless height.
With faith in yourself, you can rise and shine,
Surpassing all limits, crossing every line.
Yet in your heart, remember this truth,
The Guru's love is the essence of youth.
Like a mother's care, tender and strong,
Their wisdom will guide you, your whole life long.
You may soar high, break free and grow,
But the Guru's light will always glow.
Cherished and constant, their presence remains,
A timeless bond that forever sustains.
You have the strength to reach your own peak,
But in their embrace, it's guidance you seek.
For the Guru's teachings, pure and wise,
Are the wings that help you rise.
Faith in yourself is where the journey begins,
But the Guru's love is where it always wins.
Like a mother's hand, ever gentle, ever near,
Their wisdom will guide you through every fear.

Chapter 7

"The Gift of a Guru: Unlocking Inner Wisdom"

"Decide to Have a Guru, and He Will Appear"

In today's world, finding a moment to simply be still feels like a luxury. But this daily quiet time is essential for anyone seeking to connect with the Divine. Imagine setting aside a few minutes every day, just for yourself and for God. Away from the endless noise and distractions, these precious moments can become the foundation of a deep, personal connection to the Divine.

Modern life pulls us in so many directions. We're often surrounded by constant notifications, the pressure to achieve, and distractions that keep us from turning within. But when we deliberately carve out time for solitude, we create a space where the Divine can enter our lives. It doesn't have to be a grand ritual. Sitting quietly with closed eyes, taking gentle breaths, and letting go of the day's worries—even these small steps help us feel God's presence in a profound way.

In the journey of spirituality, however, solitude alone is only part of the path. To truly progress, we often need guidance—a teacher who has walked the path before us, someone who carries the presence of the Divine within them. This teacher, or Guru, is not simply a wise person with knowledge of scriptures or techniques; they are someone who embodies spiritual truth, who speaks from direct experience, not from theory.

Finding a true Guru is a blessing. A genuine Guru doesn't just teach—they inspire, uplift, and guide in ways that go beyond words. Being in their presence, we feel a subtle but unmistakable pull toward a higher way of being. Following their guidance with humility and dedication can transform our lives in ways we might not have imagined. But how do we know if someone is truly a Guru?

This is where our own intuition and common sense come into play. The best Gurus are those whose lives mirror their words, who don't just talk about love or humility, but live it. Trust your inner voice to help you find a teacher who feels genuine and whose presence brings peace and clarity. A true Guru guides you not just with teachings, but by the example of their own life, leading you to the Divine with love, sincerity, and grace. While they illuminate the path, it is up to each of us to walk it.

The Guru is often described as an embodiment of the Divine itself. There is a Sanskrit verse that honors the Guru as Brahma (the creator), Vishnu (the preserver), and Shiva (the destroyer of ignorance). It goes like this:

> "Guru Brahma Guru Vishnu Guru Devo Maheshwara,
> Guru Sakshat Param Brahma Tasmai Shri Gurave Namah."

This verse means, "The Guru is Brahma, the Guru is Vishnu, and the Guru is Shiva. The Guru is the Supreme Being, and to that Guru, I offer my deepest respects." In these words, the Guru is seen as all the aspects of the Divine—creating, sustaining, and transforming our spiritual journey. The Guru is a guide who helps us go beyond our limited self to the oneness of all existence.

Another beautiful saying in Sanskrit reminds us of the importance of those who guide us. It goes, *"Mata, Pita, Guru, Daivam."* This phrase means: Mother, Father, Teacher, and God. These four figures represent the foundation of our lives. Our mother and father are our first teachers, showing us love, protection, and support. The Guru, or spiritual teacher, comes next, guiding us toward wisdom and a deeper understanding of life. And finally, God—the Divine—is the ultimate destination of our journey.

The blessings of a Guru are often said to be crucial on the spiritual path. These blessings are not just words or teachings; they are a form of grace that can help us overcome inner and outer obstacles. Through their blessings, a Guru can awaken within us the courage to go deeper, the strength to face challenges, and the wisdom to find our way. This connection with a Guru, when made with love and sincerity, can accelerate our journey toward self-realization, offering insights and peace that we may never have thought possible.

In spiritual traditions, there is a concept called *diksha*, or initiation. Through diksha, a Guru transmits not only teachings but spiritual energy to the disciple. This is a sacred moment when the Guru passes on a lineage of wisdom, aligning the disciple's energy with that of the Guru. In practices like Kriya Yogam, this initiation can unlock new levels of awareness, allowing the disciple to experience life from a higher perspective. It is not merely a ceremony; it marks the start of a powerful, transformative journey.

The ultimate goal of all this guidance, all this effort, is *moksha*, or liberation—the freedom from the cycle of birth and death, from the limits of ego, and the illusions of the world. The Guru's blessings and initiation help us move toward this state of liberation. A true Guru helps to dissolve the barriers of karma and ignorance, bringing us closer to the Divine within ourselves. Through this sacred relationship with the Guru, the journey becomes not just a search for God but a discovery of God's presence in every part of our life.

This bond with the Guru can grow so deep that even distance cannot diminish it. There's a beautiful analogy in the Sai Satcharita, a text about the life of Shirdi Sai Baba, which describes the bond between the Guru and disciple. It compares this relationship to that of a mother tortoise and her young, where the mother, even from afar, lovingly gazes at her babies across the ocean. Through her mere focus, she sustains and nurtures them. Similarly, a Guru's presence can be felt even when they are not physically nearby; their love, guidance, and blessings reach us no matter where we are, nourishing our spirit and protecting us on the path.

Learning from a Guru is a cornerstone of Kriya Yogam, as the Guru imparts not only the techniques but the essence of the practice. Through their guidance, we can understand the subtler aspects of Kriya and receive support when challenges arise. With trust, patience, and humility, we can grow in our understanding and devotion, moving closer to the ultimate goal of self-realization.

In this tradition, the Guru-disciple relationship is sacred, and certain principles help keep it strong:

1. **Understand the Role of the Guru**: A Guru isn't merely a teacher but a spiritual guide, helping us move beyond the ego to a deeper truth.
2. **Seek Authentic Initiation**: Kriya Yogam practices require precise guidance. A genuine Guru ensures that teachings are preserved and transmitted with integrity.
3. **Follow Instructions Faithfully**: The Guru's methods are crafted for our growth; altering techniques can hinder progress.
4. **Keep an Open Heart**: Humility and openness allow us to receive the Guru's wisdom without the interference of ego.
5. **Stay Connected with the Guru**: Whether in person or through correspondence, sharing experiences helps the Guru guide us more effectively.
6. **Have Patience**: Spiritual growth is gradual; trust that the Guru's teachings are shaping you for long-term progress.
7. **Embrace Reverence**: Respect and gratitude strengthen the bond with the Guru, allowing the teachings to resonate more deeply.
8. **Avoid Multiple Gurus**: In Kriya Yogam, it is usually best to follow one Guru or lineage to avoid confusion and preserve focus.

A verse called *Guru Ashtakam*, composed by Adi Shankaracharya, captures the essence of reverence for the Guru. In it, each verse is a humble reminder that the Guru is not only a teacher but the very embodiment of the Divine, leading us toward liberation.

We also find guidance in simple, heartfelt mantras like *Aum Hreem Shree Gurubhyo Namaha*, which translates as a salutation to the Guru, honoring the divine energy that the Guru represents. Through such mantras, we express gratitude for the light they bring to our journey.

As we take each step on this path, we learn that the Guru's presence is a gift, guiding us with love and wisdom. It's a bond that carries us closer to the truth of who we are and the joy of being one with the Divine. This relationship, nurtured with devotion and care, becomes the key that unlocks the door to self-realization and freedom.

Kriya Amrutham 8

When you start

your morning

with Kriya,

you'll notice that the rest of your day flows effortlessly,

and things seem to fall into

place naturally.

Chapter 8

Kriya Yogam Do's and Don'ts

Kriya Yogam is a profound spiritual practice aimed at accelerating self-realization and union with the Divine. It involves various techniques, primarily focused on controlling the breath (pranayama), concentration (dharana), and meditation (dhyana). As with any advanced spiritual discipline, there are certain guidelines (do's and don'ts) that help maintain the integrity of the practice, ensure the safety of the practitioner, and deepen the transformative effects. Below is a comprehensive list of the essential do's and don'ts for Kriya Yogis:

Do's for Kriya Yogis:

Do Learn from a Guru (Teacher) properly:

Guidance from a Guru or an experienced teacher is invaluable in Kriya Yogam.

Do practice regularly:

Consistency is crucial in Kriya Yogam. Establish a daily practice that aligns with your schedule. A fixed time, preferably early in the morning, ensures a disciplined approach. Even if it's just for a short duration, the regularity is important.

Do practice with devotion:

Approach Kriya Yogam with sincerity, faith, and reverence for the Divine. The intention behind the practice must be pure and focused on self-realization and inner peace, not worldly gains.

Do maintain a balanced lifestyle:

Kriya Yogam requires a balance of physical health, mental clarity, and emotional stability. A yogi should follow a disciplined life with moderation in eating, sleeping, and socializing. This balance enhances the effectiveness of the practice.

Do respect your body and mind:

Kriya Yogam can be physically intense, especially for beginners. Listen to your body's limits and practice with mindfulness. Overexertion can lead to fatigue or injury. It's important to build up gradually and not push beyond your limits.

Do stay grounded in humility:

Humility is essential. Kriya Yogam is a tool for personal growth, not ego enhancement. Be open to learning from experienced teachers and fellow practitioners. Recognize that the path is long and requires patience.

Do follow a vegetarian diet:

While not an absolute rule for all, many advanced Kriya Yogis recommend a vegetarian diet as it promotes physical lightness, mental clarity, and a compassionate attitude, which is in alignment with the yogic lifestyle.

Do meditate daily:

Meditation is the heart of Kriya Yogam. The primary goal of Kriya Yogam is to still the mind and develop deep inner awareness. Practicing meditation regularly helps increase focus, clarity, and inner peace.

Do practice proper pranayama (breathing exercises):

Pranayama is a cornerstone of Kriya Yogam. Techniques like alternate nostril breathing, kapalbhati, and others help balance prana (life energy), improve concentration, and purify the mind.

Do cultivate detachment (Vairagya):

Kriya Yogis work towards detachment from the material world. Practice non-attachment to outcomes, desires, and external circumstances. This does not mean renouncing the world but developing a healthy relationship with it, free of dependency.

Do develop self-discipline (Tapas):

Tapas, or self-discipline, is crucial in Kriya Yogam. This includes both outer discipline (regular practice, ethical behavior) and inner discipline (mental control, focus).

Don'ts for Kriya Yogis:

Don't practice in a distracted or unfocused state:

Kriya Yogam requires deep concentration and focus. Avoid practicing when you are physically or mentally tired, distracted, or under stress. These conditions will hinder the depth of your practice.

Don't overindulge in food, sleep, or material pleasures:

A Kriya Yogi must avoid excessive indulgence in food, sleep, or sensory pleasures, as these can lead to imbalances and hinder spiritual progress. Practice moderation in all aspects of life.

Don't practice Kriya Yogam with an egoistic mindset:

The goal of Kriya Yogam is self-realization and spiritual growth, not the enhancement of one's ego. Avoid practicing for show, seeking fame, or using the techniques to manipulate others.

Don't skip proper guidance:

Kriya Yogam is a deep and transformative science that requires proper initiation and guidance. Never attempt to learn advanced techniques without the guidance of an experienced teacher or master. Incorrect practice can be harmful.

Don't force the body or mind:

Yoga, particularly Kriya Yogam, is about gentle refinement, not force. Do not strain during practice. If you feel physical discomfort or mental unrest, take a step back and proceed with care.

Don't engage in negative or harmful thoughts:

The mental state is equally important as the physical. A Kriya Yogi should avoid negative emotions, thoughts, or harmful actions. Cultivate positivity, love, compassion, and understanding. Negative mental states disrupt the flow of energy and impede progress.

Don't neglect your physical health:

While the focus of Kriya Yogam is on the mind and spirit, neglecting the physical body can lead to issues that distract from the practice. Ensure that you take care of your health through proper nutrition, exercise, and rest.

Don't rush the process:

Spiritual progress takes time. Kriya Yogam is not about achieving quick results or becoming enlightened overnight. It is a gradual process that unfolds over years of disciplined practice. Avoid impatience and trust the process.

Don't try to force extraordinary experiences:

Many people enter Kriya Yogam expecting mystical experiences, but this can create attachment to the experiences rather than focusing on the true goal of self-realization. Do not force experiences, and do not be discouraged if you don't feel dramatic changes immediately.

Don't get attached to the results of your practice:

Kriya Yogam requires non-attachment to outcomes. While the practice brings transformation, it is important not to be overly focused on specific results like worldly success, health improvements, or altered states of consciousness. The aim is inner peace, not external validation.

The practice of Kriya Yogam is a path of inner purification and spiritual awakening. By adhering to these do's and don'ts, a practitioner can maintain a balanced and progressive approach to the practice. The transformative potential of Kriya Yogam can be fully realized when practiced with consistency, humility, and devotion, with the ultimate goal of attaining oneness with the Divine.

Kriya Amrutham 9

Kriya Yogam holds the potential to heal even the most challenging health conditions like AIDS, cancer, diabetes, asthma, high blood pressure, and arthritis.

It can bring peace to the mind, freeing people from issues like phobias, stress, insomnia, anger, irritation, and even extreme mental struggles.

Kriya Yogam helps overcome addictions to substances like alcohol, drugs like opium, heroin, tobacco, and cigarettes.

On a deeper level, it offers spiritual awakening, helping you understand your past and navigate the present with clarity.

For students, it boosts focus, memory, and learning abilities.

By practicing Kriya Yogam, one can balance the spiritual and material worlds, ultimately achieving moksha—liberation—in this very life.

With love and care, Kriya Yogam invites everyone to experience this transformative path for a healthier, happier, and more enlightened life.

Chapter 9

Benefits of doing Kriya Yogam

Kriya Yogam is more than just a form of exercise or meditation—it's a doorway into a life filled with peace, vitality, and clarity. By practicing specific techniques, Kriya Yogam allows your breath, heart, and thoughts to slow down naturally, calming the mind and grounding you in a deeply satisfying inner peace.

As you continue with the practice, you start to feel more alert, joyful, and aware. It's like finding a special kind of happiness, one that lasts longer than regular pleasures. This joy comes from a sense of connection—to yourself, to others, and to something bigger than all of us. Kriya Yogam gently guides you to see the world with fresh eyes and a calm heart.

There's a belief in Kriya Yogam that human life is precious, almost like a gift from the divine. Kriya Yogam respects this human-divine connection and uses practices that draw out the best in us. Through breathwork, meditation, and self-discipline, this path aligns the body, mind, and soul, raising our awareness closer to a divine state of being.

The idea is simple yet powerful: the divine isn't something far away; it lives within each of us. Practicing Kriya Yogam helps to awaken this divine essence, bringing us closer to the ultimate goal—feeling connected to all of life. This journey bridges the gap between our daily lives and a higher spiritual consciousness, honoring both human and divine existence.

In Kriya Yogam, karma—the effects of our past actions—is central. Many events in our lives are shaped by karma from previous lives, which influences our experiences, opportunities, and challenges today. Kriya Yogam shows us that this karma, whether positive or negative, impacts all aspects of our present life.

If you have practiced Kriya Yogam in past lives, you might feel a natural pull toward it in this life, as if resuming an old journey. This sense of familiarity reflects the idea that spiritual growth is a continuous process, with each life building upon the last. Kriya Yogam offers us a way to understand our karma, transforming and healing past patterns so we can move forward with greater clarity.

A deep practice of Kriya Yogam can unlock hidden insights, including memories or visions of past lives. By awakening these memories, practitioners gain a wider perspective on their journey and a clearer understanding of how their past shapes their present. This awareness brings a sense of peace and purpose, helping practitioners make sense of life's patterns and ultimately guiding them toward liberation.

One of the transformative experiences in Kriya Yogam involves focusing on a specific point between the eyebrows, known as the third eye or spiritual eye. As practitioners progress, they might see a light at this point, which symbolizes a higher state of consciousness and a deeper awareness. This light is more than just an image—it's a doorway to understanding oneself and the universe on a profound level.

This experience is often described as deeply calming, clearing the mind of worries and distractions. Focusing on this light awakens a state known as *Gyanaozhi*, a spiritual awareness where we see beyond ordinary reality and connect with Universal Consciousness. In this state, we feel one with all existence, stepping beyond the ego and embracing our true, divine nature. Kriya Yogam purifies the mind, lifting us towards wisdom, enlightenment, and liberation.

When life presents hardships, Kriya Yogam offers a way to find peace and strength. This practice can be a powerful source of healing and guidance, helping us handle life's challenges with resilience and spiritual insight. It creates a bridge to our innermost self, providing clarity and wisdom that reach beyond ordinary thinking.

One of the core lessons in Kriya Yogam is letting go of negative emotions, like anger and ego, which often cloud our minds and block our path. These emotions limit us by preventing positive energy from flowing freely, keeping us from connecting with our higher self. Practicing Kriya

Yogam helps us release anger and ego, creating an open, receptive space for deeper meditation and spiritual growth.

An important teaching of Kriya Yogam is that God exists within us, not just in physical objects. If someone gives you a symbol of God and someone else asks for it, give it freely. Remember, God's presence is with you always in your heart, not limited to any material form.

Holding onto things can sometimes create attachment and lead to suffering. Practicing generosity and detachment brings peace, reminding us that divine presence and blessings are everywhere, unlimited and abundant. By letting go, we create space for inner peace and spiritual growth, aligning ourselves with the higher principles of Kriya Yogam.

When anger and ego fade, our minds naturally become calmer and clearer, opening the door to a deeper connection with ourselves and the universe. Practicing Kriya Yogam transforms us from within, bringing us closer to a state of pure awareness and enlightenment.

Regular practice of Kriya Yogam doesn't just create inner peace; it also brings vitality and joy that reflect outwardly as a youthful, vibrant energy. This practice harmonizes the body, mind, and spirit, creating a sense of well-being that radiates through every aspect of life.

One of the key teachings of Kriya Yogam is the constant remembrance that God is always with us, providing strength and comfort. This awareness reinforces our faith, guiding us with trust and a sense of security in divine guidance. This is the transformative power of Kriya Yogam—to let go, trust in the divine, and allow spiritual growth to happen naturally.

As we practice, we reach a level where life begins to flow more easily. By surrendering control and letting the practice guide us, we release obstacles that might block our path. Kriya Yogam leads us to a life of spiritual awareness, gently and steadily opening the way to peace and fulfillment.

To deepen this journey, Kriya Yogam includes advanced practices like Maha Mandiram, a technique to deepen meditation. Some practitioners may see colors during meditation, beginning with black and shifting to blue, representing the mind's entry into deeper consciousness. Chanting "Om Namah Shivaya" invokes divine energy, filling the mind with focus and aligning it with the sacred.

Another practice is *Manam Adaganum*, the control of the mind. Observing silence, known as *Mouna Vratha*, is a powerful way to calm and focus the mind, reducing distractions and cultivating peace. Acts of charity, or *Dhana Dharma*, help purify the heart and mind, removing selfishness and fostering compassion. By integrating silence, charity, and mantra chanting, Kriya Yogam brings us to a higher level of awareness and spiritual depth.

Reflecting daily on life's blessings is a valuable part of Kriya Yogam, reminding us to honor the good in our lives. Setting aside quiet time for introspection, especially in a dark room with closed eyes, lets us explore our inner self and understand our role in the world. This time of reflection is a chance to listen to our soul, deepening our connection to it.

Anger, which often comes from unmet expectations or poor communication, can be seen with new clarity. Recognizing this helps us cultivate better relationships and emotional well-being. The ego, like a small needle in butter, can creep in and quietly undermine our humility. Kriya Yogam teaches us to be mindful of this, helping us remain humble and centered as we navigate life's challenges.

As we grow in wisdom, we learn that life's journey is fleeting, and that true greatness lies in humility and service. Recognizing our small place in the vast universe brings a natural humility that enriches our lives.

Kriya Yogam reminds us of our interdependence on the elements—earth, water, fire, air, and space. Acknowledging this brings gratitude for the world around us and helps us see ourselves as part of a greater whole. By surrendering to the divine, with humility and gratitude, we transcend the ego's hold and connect with our divine essence.

Through humility, gratitude, and self-reflection, Kriya Yogam brings us closer to ourselves and to the divine. This journey helps us understand our place in the world, deepening our spiritual connection and guiding us toward greater awareness.

When we finally let go and surrender, life begins to flow with ease. We no longer feel the need to control everything, trusting instead that the universe is supporting us. By doing our best with joy and sincerity, we align with divine flow, inviting a life of peace, spiritual growth, and the profound fulfillment that comes with discovering our true selves.

Kriya Yogam is ultimately about living in harmony with ourselves and the universe, transforming us into radiant, peaceful beings in tune with all that is divine.

Kriya Amrutham 10

Don't hurt yourself and Don't hurt others

1. *Put love into everything you do: Without love, your actions will feel empty, and life loses its meaning. Let love guide your thoughts and deeds.*
2. *What goes around comes around: Every action creates a ripple. What you send out into the world will eventually return to you. Choose kindness, compassion, and honesty over harm or selfishness.*
3. *Think before you act: Every action has a reaction. Before making a decision, pause and ask yourself—will this bring harm or healing? Avoid actions you'll regret later.*
4. *You are your own best friend: No one knows you better than you. Be kind to yourself, support your growth, and guide yourself with wisdom.*
5. *Take 5 minutes daily to talk to yourself: Reflect on your day, your thoughts, and your choices. This daily conversation helps you stay centered, aware, and aligned with your best self.*
6. *Own your actions: Life is about responsibility. Accept the consequences of your choices with courage, whether they bring joy or lessons.*
7. *Avoid creating suffering: Stop doing things that harm your body, mind, or soul. Acting against yourself only brings unnecessary pain.*
8. *Live wisely and mindfully: Don't let today's thrill turn into tomorrow's regret. Let your choices reflect awareness and thoughtfulness.*
9. *Be consistent and intentional: What feels like everything today shouldn't make you feel foolish tomorrow. Build a life that grows in value every day.*
10. *Stay connected to your truth: Talk to yourself, reflect, and make choices that align with your highest good. A mindful and sensible life will bring peace and pride not just to you but even to the Creator.*

Chapter 10

Karma Sidhantham

We don't know what karma we did in our past life, but in this life, spiritual knowledge is definitely needed to live a good life.

Karma is the ability to know through experience. When one realizes who they truly are, the nature of karma disappears.

In daily life, we often see people enduring struggles for things they feel they lack—health, wealth, love, and more. To gain these, many find themselves caught up in an endless, often lonely, pursuit within a world driven by materialism. But why must this struggle exist? Why can't everyone have what they need and find happiness? What went wrong? Why did God create a world of "haves" and "have-nots"?

In the journey of life, each of us is essentially alone, from birth to death. Who we are today is shaped by our past actions, and the choices we make now lay the foundation for our future. Whether born into a large, supportive family or facing life's challenges alone, our personal journey remains uniquely ours.

Loved ones can't bear our karma; each soul is here to cleanse and evolve. This purification is a gradual process, sometimes stretching across lifetimes, shaped by our deeds of kindness and sacrifice. This journey, called soul evolution, can ultimately reshape our destiny. Living with purpose, striving for excellence, and aiming for a higher destiny leads to mukthi, or liberation, freeing the soul from the cycle of birth and death.

In life, when we rely on nature's simple, God-given resources, we find clarity and peace. Everything else—the man-made attractions and endless artificial comforts—can be an illusion, pulling us away from true purpose. Instead of reacting to the constant demands and pressures of modern society, it's wiser to live guided by the principles of the heart.

Young minds are especially vulnerable to the powerful pull of today's world, often unaware that self-mastery can be surprisingly simple. Let's explore how to step away from these distractions to live a fulfilled life, complete with health, wealth, and genuine happiness.

Throughout the soul's journey across many lifetimes, we accumulate marks, or impressions, from past actions that we call sins. These impressions shape our identity, influencing the choices we make and the consequences that follow—what we call karma. Imagine if we could cleanse our souls of these impressions, Doing so would lighten our burdens, ease our struggles, and unlock new possibilities for growth and fulfillment.

This book serves as a guide to help clear these impressions from our souls, reduce the weight of our karma, and create a better destiny. By transforming our karma, we can open the way to a more joyful, prosperous, and balanced life.

To change our karma, we must begin by understanding who we truly are. While we often have a sense of our physical and material selves, knowing our true nature requires exploring our inner psychology.

We tend to believe that our conscious mind directs all our actions, but in reality, about ninety percent of our actions are shaped by the subconscious. To bring real change, we need to look inward and understand the deeper layers of our mind—our beliefs, habitual thoughts, and hidden motivations. Only when we gain at least an eighty per cent awareness of these subconscious patterns can true transformation begin, as real change must come from within, not from external influences.

Exploring our thought processes, becoming deeply aware of our minds, is the essence of meditation. Meditation helps us observe our thoughts and actions without bias, seeing ourselves as we truly are. It shows us where to begin the work. Once we focus on transforming our inner world, the external world will naturally begin to shift in alignment with this inner change. We don't have to force it; as we evolve inwardly, the outer world follows effortlessly.

Purpose of Life:

Help people see that there is more suffering in life than what we usually see in our everyday world. Don't limit yourself to just the five senses—there is so much more, and the spark within you is part of a greater, mysterious self. Understand this, learn it, and help others learn it too, bringing more people into this way of life.

Suffering often leads people to become spiritual. There isn't only one path to follow, but always remember that inner awakening is essential. In the journey of growth, we have evolved from single cells to human beings, and from here, our growth should be spiritual.

Is everything in life predetermined?

Not exactly. Life's events aren't strictly predetermined; they are the natural outcomes of our actions. Often, it seems as though our fate is fixed because we only see the effects, not the causes.

According to the law of karma, every effect has a cause. While we can't change past actions, the present moment offers us the freedom to shape our future. So, although there may be some underlying patterns or "blueprints," we are not bound by a fully fixed fate.

If everything were predetermined, we wouldn't need to put in any effort. In my view, while there are certain boundaries the mind can't transcend, within those limits there is vast potential. It's up to us to explore this potential. Simply accepting life as "fate" and doing nothing will lead nowhere.

In your efforts, remember that the mind and body have their limits, and external conditions like nature and natural events are beyond our control. However, our minds are within our influence. This is where sadhana and spiritual practices come in—to help us master the mind. The beauty of mastering the mind is that, as we delve deeper, we can release it from its limitations. When the mind touches the infinite, it transcends karma and moves beyond worldly concerns. That freedom is not predetermined.

Remind yourself: there is always an opening, always a way forward.

How are memories carried with us from one life to the next?

While our physical brain holds memories during a lifetime, these memories don't vanish when we die. Rather than being stored solely in brain cells, memories are imprinted within the sukshma sharira, or subtle body. This subtle body accompanies the soul from life to life, carrying impressions like a breeze that retains the scent of flowers.

As described in the Bhagavad Gita, this subtle body holds all accumulated memories, influencing the nature of our next birth and our karmic journey forward. We carry these impressions deep within, even if they're not consciously accessible in everyday life. It is said that, at the moment of death, many recall their past lives in a rapid, vivid sequence.

In the Gita, Krishna tells Arjuna, "You and I have both been born many times; the difference is, I remember, and you do not." This doesn't mean that our past experiences are lost; they remain within the soul's subtle layers, guiding us forward in our journey.

The Principles of Destiny:

Destiny is something we can shape actively, starting with three core principles:

1. The Power of the Present

The most vital principle of destiny is that change is only possible in the present. The past is beyond our reach and cannot be altered, so dwelling on it only wastes precious energy. Instead, we can focus on clearing the past's impressions, erasing the blueprints it left, and focusing on today. The choices we make in each present moment shape our future, making each day an opportunity to design a brighter trajectory.

2. The Influence of Our Thoughts

we shape our destiny not only through actions but also through our thoughts—our desires, attractions, and aversions. Notice how some things pull us in, while others repel us or leave us indifferent.

Our likes attract certain experiences to us, while our dislikes can also bind us strongly, though in a negative way.

Most of our thoughts are wrapped up in these unconscious reactions of likes and dislikes: "I love that house and want it," "I don't want to work with him," or "She's so beautiful; I wish I looked like her." These thoughts continuously create impressions in our minds. By reacting with awareness instead of reflex, we gain greater control over our destiny.

3. Collective Evolution

Destiny isn't just an individual path; it's also a shared journey. We are co-evolving with humanity and the communities around us.

While we may strive to improve the world through politics, social movements, or community causes, true change starts with personal transformation. Tolstoy wisely said, "Everyone thinks of changing the world, but no one thinks of changing himself." By evolving ourselves first, we can contribute meaningfully to the broader evolution of humanity, shifting the collective destiny in a positive direction.

The Importance of Training the Mind

Many of us let our minds wander without direction and react quickly to things happening around us. When we do this, we give up control of our lives to what happens outside us. So, how can we change this? By training our minds, we make them stronger and better able to shape our future.

Who helps us make this change?

No one. Just like a river finds its own path, we must make our own way.

Meditation is important for this, Meditation helps us control our thoughts, find peace inside, and connect with our inner wisdom, which can guide us in life.

You might feel happy as you are now, but ask yourself: Is this happiness coming from outside things?

True and lasting happiness comes from building inner strength so that you stay calm and happy no matter what happens in life. Remember, nature's powers are with you.

Where Is Destiny Taking Us?

When we talk about "destiny," we're often referring to a path that feels beyond us, as if we're being led somewhere. This idea can sometimes make us wonder if we even have control over where we end up. If our future were set in stone, after all, would our own dreams, goals, or choices mean anything?

However, destiny isn't a rigid, predetermined track. Instead, it's more like a river that flows, responding to the shape of the land, the strength of the currents, and the elements surrounding it. Our thoughts, choices, and actions act like currents or rocks in this river, influencing its direction and shape.

Each day, what we focus on, the actions we take, and the values we hold close all guide the direction of our lives.

When we recognize this, we start to understand that we're not just passive riders along a set course. We are co-creators with life itself.

By embracing a proactive approach—one where we align our intentions, grow in awareness, and make mindful choices—we gain a say in shaping our lives. This shift is powerful because it's not just about reaching our own personal goals. It's also about contributing to the world's overall direction.

When we live intentionally and make choices aligned with growth, kindness, and purpose, we set a positive example. This influence can inspire others to do the same, creating a ripple effect.

In this way, our "destiny" is not just about where we end up but about the impact we leave on the world. Life isn't just something that happens to us; it's something we actively shape, day by day. By taking conscious steps, we find meaning in each moment and create a future aligned with our highest values.

How to Clear Past Karmas and Cultivate Inner Freedom

Freeing oneself from past karma is a journey of gratitude, generosity, and humility that deepens our connection to life and helps us live in harmony with the universe. Through simple yet profound practices, we can release karmic burdens and embrace a life of inner peace. Here's a guide to clearing past karma:

1. Thank and Give: Building a Relationship with the Pancha Bhutas (Five Elements)

The Pancha Bhutas—Earth, Water, Fire, Air, and Space—are the foundations of life. Everything in our world is born of these elements, and they sustain us every day. Cultivating a deep respect and appreciation for them is the first step in releasing past karma.

- **Thank the Elements**: Take a moment each day to recognize and silently thank the elements for their support and balance. Acknowledge their role in your life, from the air you breathe to the water you drink.
- **Receive with Gratitude**: Recognize that everything you receive is a blessing from the Pancha Bhutas. This gratitude aligns your life with the natural flow, allowing things to unfold more effortlessly.
- **Return the Gift**: Give back what you have received. Share your blessings with others, be it kindness, support, or material resources. This creates a beautiful cycle of giving and receiving, bringing abundance to both you and those around you.
- **Continual Cycle of Generosity**: As the universe recognizes your acts of kindness, it will respond by blessing you with even more abundance. This positive cycle helps dissolve past karmic imprints, creating a life filled with grace and flow.

2. Anna Dhanam: Offering Food to Those in Need

Giving food, or Anna Dhanam, is a profound act of compassion. When we offer food to others, we help nourish their bodies and souls. This simple act of generosity creates a ripple effect of positive karma that returns to us as blessings. Sharing a meal with those who need it most helps ease karmic burdens and strengthens our connection to humanity.

3. Keep Food for Birds

Placing food out for birds reflects a respect for all life. Birds remind us of freedom and lightness, and by feeding them, we reinforce a connection to the natural world. This act of caring for small creatures brings balance to our karmic energy, as it fosters a larger compassion for all beings.

4. Feed Dogs

Feeding stray dogs is another form of generosity. Dogs are often seen as loyal protectors and companions, and by caring for them, we practice kindness. This small act is both a blessing to the animals and a spiritual offering that helps cleanse karmic residues, filling our hearts with compassion and kindness.

5. Give Money to Beggars

Helping those in financial need by offering even a small amount of money softens our hearts and reduces karmic baggage. This practice teaches humility and empathy, reminding us that every act of kindness counts. Each small gesture of support helps lighten the karmic load we carry.

6. Express Gratitude for Everything

Gratitude is the foundation of spiritual life, and expressing it regularly can dissolve negative karmic patterns. Make it a habit to thank everyone and everything, from loved ones to strangers, and for every blessing you receive. A simple "Nannri" (Thank You) or "Vaazgh Valamudan" (Live with Prosperity) expresses your appreciation and spreads positivity. By keeping gratitude at the center of your life, you create an aura of abundance and happiness that dissolves past karma.

These practices, rooted in love and selflessness, build positive karma and bring peace and clarity into our lives. Practicing gratitude and kindness consistently nurtures good karma and aligns us with the universe's natural harmony. By letting go of karmic weight, we make space for joy, freedom, and a deeper spiritual connection.

Nannri. Vaazgh Valamudan.

Kriya Amrutham 11

The Pancha Bhutas (earth, water, fire, air, and ether) and the Seven Chakras are key to understanding the harmony between the human body and the cosmos.

Each chakra governs specific energies and is connected to the elements, influencing physical, emotional, and spiritual well-being.

In Kriya Yogam, balancing the elements and activating the chakras purifies the body, awakens latent energies, and elevates consciousness.

The ascent of Kundalini through the chakras transforms the practitioner, aligning them with universal forces and leading to spiritual realization.

This chapter explores how mastering these energies unveils the profound connection between the microcosm within and the infinite universe.

Chapter 11

Pancha Bhutas and Seven Chakras

In Kriya Yogam, one of the core idea is understanding how the body and mind are connected to the universe through two major concepts: the **Pancha Bhutas** (the Five Great Elements) and the **Seven Chakras** (energy centers). These ideas are crucial because they help practitioners purify, transform, and awaken the spiritual energy within themselves.

The Pancha Bhutas (The Five Great Elements)

The Pancha Bhutas are the five elements that make up everything around us—Earth, Water, Fire, Air, and Ether (or Space). These elements aren't just part of the world outside; they're also inside each of us, influencing both our physical and energetic states. In Kriya Yogam, understanding and balancing these elements is key because it helps harmonize our inner world, setting the stage for spiritual awakening.

1. **Earth (Prithvi):**
   - The Earth element represents stability and grounding. It's the solid part of life, linked to the body's bones, muscles, and tissues.
   - When the Earth element is balanced, a Kriya Yogi feels stable and rooted, both physically and mentally. This stability is vital for deep meditation and inner peace.

2. **Water (Apas):**
   - Water is fluid, nourishing, and adaptable. It's connected to our emotions, creativity, and even our reproductive system.
   - By balancing Water, Kriya Yogis can better manage their emotions and stay adaptable when faced with life's ups and downs.

3. **Fire (Agni):**
   - Fire is all about transformation. It represents energy, purification, and the ability to change. It governs digestion, metabolism, and mental clarity.
   - For a yogi, balancing Fire is essential because it helps purify the body and mind, transforming lower energies into spiritual energy that fuels growth and clarity.

4. **Air (Vayu):**
   - Air is linked to movement, freedom, and the breath. It governs the nervous system and how we think.
   - Mastering the Air element through breath control (pranayama) is a powerful tool for directing the life force, or prana, upwards through the body, stimulating spiritual awakening.

5. **Ether (Akasha):**
   - Ether, or Space, is the most subtle of all elements. It represents the vastness and openness of the mind, intuition, and higher consciousness.
   - In Kriya Yogam, working with Ether helps the practitioner experience expanded states of awareness, where they can connect with higher dimensions of spiritual consciousness.

Each of these elements has its own unique role in our bodies, and when we balance them, it helps us unlock higher levels of awareness and spiritual potential. These elements are also connected to specific **chakras**, or energy centers, which are key to spiritual growth.

The Seven Chakras (Energy Centers)

The Seven Chakras are energy centers that run along the spine, from the base all the way to the crown of the head. Each chakra is linked to different physical, emotional, and spiritual aspects of our being. In Kriya Yogam, progress is made by awakening and energizing these chakras, helping prana (life force energy) rise through the body and unlock deeper states of awareness.

1. **Muladhara Chakra (Root Chakra):**
   - **Location:** Base of the spine
   - **Element:** Earth
   - **Attributes:** Survival, stability, grounding
   - **Purpose in Kriya Yogam:** This is the foundation of your energy system. The Root Chakra holds the dormant Kundalini energy. Awakening this chakra releases blockages and allows energy to move upwards, marking the first steps in your spiritual journey.

2. **Svadhisthana Chakra (Sacral Chakra):**
   - **Location:** Lower abdomen, just below the navel
   - **Element:** Water
   - **Attributes:** Creativity, sexuality, emotional balance
   - **Purpose in Kriya Yogam:** The Sacral Chakra governs emotional flow and creativity. By balancing this chakra, you gain control over your emotions and desires, creating inner harmony.
3. **Manipura Chakra (Solar Plexus Chakra):**
   - **Location:** Solar plexus, above the navel
   - **Element:** Fire
   - **Attributes:** Willpower, confidence, personal power
   - **Purpose in Kriya Yogam:** This chakra is where your personal power resides. Awakening it transforms lower energies into higher spiritual energies, helping you grow in willpower and inner strength.
4. **Anahata Chakra (Heart Chakra):**
   - **Location:** Center of the chest
   - **Element:** Air
   - **Attributes:** Love, compassion, harmony
   - **Purpose in Kriya Yogam:** The Heart Chakra is the bridge between the physical and spiritual realms. Opening this chakra expands your capacity for love, compassion, and peace, helping you transcend ego and connect to selfless love.
5. **Vishuddha Chakra (Throat Chakra):**
   - **Location:** Throat
   - **Element:** Ether
   - **Attributes:** Communication, truth, purity
   - **Purpose in Kriya Yogam:** The Throat Chakra is your center of self-expression. Awakening it allows you to speak your truth with clarity and communicate in alignment with your higher purpose.

6. **Ajna Chakra (Third Eye Chakra):**
   - **Location:** Between the eyebrows
   - **Element:** None (associated with mind and light)
   - **Attributes:** Intuition, wisdom, clarity
   - **Purpose in Kriya Yogam:** The Third Eye Chakra is your seat of intuition and spiritual insight. When it opens, you begin to see beyond ordinary reality, gaining access to deeper spiritual truths.
7. **Sahasrara Chakra (Crown Chakra):**
   - **Location:** Top of the head
   - **Element:** Beyond elements (pure consciousness)
   - **Attributes:** Enlightenment, unity with the Divine, liberation
   - **Purpose in Kriya Yogam:** The Crown Chakra is the highest energy center, where ultimate spiritual enlightenment and unity with the Divine occur. When fully awakened, it brings liberation, dissolving the sense of separation and connecting you with the universal consciousness.

The Role of Pancha Bhutas and Chakras in Kriya Yogam Practice

In Kriya Yogam, the goal is to purify and activate each of these chakras so prana can flow freely through the body. This is done through techniques like **pranayama** (breath control), **visualization**, and **mantras**. By balancing the Pancha Bhutas within, the yogi creates harmony between the body and mind, preparing for deeper meditation.

Here's how the process works:

1. **Purification of Elements:** By balancing the Pancha Bhutas through lifestyle, diet, meditation, and breathing exercise, the yogi creates a harmonious internal environment where energy can rise and expand.

2. **Chakra Activation:** Using focused techniques, the yogi activates each chakra one by one. As energy rises from the Root to the Crown, the practitioner gains deeper awareness and spiritual insight at each stage.
3. **Union with the Divine:** The ultimate goal of this practice is to reach the Crown Chakra, where the yogi experiences oneness with the Divine, transcending the ego and merging with universal consciousness.

The journey through the Pancha Bhutas and Seven Chakras is transformative in Kriya Yogam. By working with these elements and energy centers, practitioners can accelerate their spiritual growth, deepen their self-awareness, and ultimately experience the liberation that comes with enlightenment. This path isn't just about understanding the body and mind—it's about unlocking the divine potential within, leading to ultimate freedom and unity with the universe.

Kriya Amrutham 12

Being Close to Nature

Nature is not just a backdrop to our lives but a profound teacher and source of healing. In Kriya Yogam, being close to nature is seen as essential for harmonizing the mind, body, and soul. The Pancha Bhutas (five elements) that form the universe also shape our bodies, making our connection to nature deeply intrinsic.

Advanced Kriya practices often involve tuning into nature's rhythms—such as the breath of the wind, the stillness of mountains, or the flow of rivers—to deepen meditation and spiritual awareness. Spending time in natural environments helps quiet the mind, purify energies, and awaken inner harmony.

This chapter highlights the transformative power of aligning with nature, reminding us that living in tune with the Earth nurtures not only physical vitality but also spiritual growth, fostering a deeper connection to the divine.

Chapter 12

Introduction to Being Close to Nature

Many spiritual traditions and philosophers, both old and new, share a profound insight: humans were meant to live in harmony with nature. Over time, though, we've drifted away from that connection, primarily in the name of progress. It's not just an abstract idea; it's a theme that appears in both Eastern and Western thought, showing how our detachment from the natural world may be a root cause of many of our physical, emotional, and spiritual problems.

Take, for example, the wisdom shared by the **Siddhars** and the teachings of **Kriya Yogam**. These spiritual practices emphasize that true well-being comes when we align ourselves with the natural rhythms of the universe. It's about reconnecting with the natural state of being we're all born with—a state that's often disrupted by modern living. In this worldview, human beings are an intrinsic part of the cosmic order, and separation from nature leads to imbalance, illness, and suffering.

This idea also echoes in modern environmental thought. The loss of our connection to the Earth is seen as a major factor in physical and mental health decline. Technology, urbanization, and industrialization have created a barrier between us and the natural world, and as a result, our bodies and minds suffer.

When you think about it, it makes sense. As human civilization advanced, we became more focused on building complex systems—cities, technologies, industries—and in doing so, we neglected the simple, natural laws that govern our well-being. Things like processed foods, synthetic environments, and the constant stress of modern life have thrown us off balance.

Spiritual practices, especially those in traditions like **Kriya Yogam** and **Ayurveda**, teach us to reconnect with nature. Take **Pranayama** for instance. This practice is rooted in the natural rhythms of breath and the environment. By regulating the breath, practitioners learn to bring their body and energy into harmony with the world around them.

The message here is clear: While civilization has undoubtedly made life more convenient in many ways, true health and happiness may come from returning to simpler ways of living. It's about honoring the body as part of nature, and recognizing the interconnectedness of all life.

"Andathil irupadu, pindathil iruku"

(ஆண்டத்தில் இருப்பது, பிண்டத்தில் இருக்கு)

This is a profound Tamil spiritual expression, which translates to: **"What exists in the universe, exists in the individual."**

This phrase captures a powerful concept known as the **microcosm-macrocosm connection**. It means that the entire universe, with all its energies and forces, is mirrored within each human being. The universe is not separate from us; we are intrinsically connected to it. The energies that shape the stars, the planets, and the galaxies also flow within us.

In spiritual traditions like **Shaiva Siddhanta** and **Tantra**, and particularly in **Kriya Yogam**, this connection is key. It suggests that the divine is not something external to us, but something that resides within. The energy, the principles that govern the universe, are all contained within the human body. This understanding leads to the realization that **the soul of the individual is the same as the universal soul**, or **Brahman**, a central idea in **Vedanta philosophy**.

Recognizing this connection brings a deep sense of peace and clarity. It helps a seeker realize that spiritual enlightenment and self-realization are not external pursuits but internal awakenings. When we cultivate inner purity and align ourselves with the cosmic energies—through practices like **Kriya Yogam** and meditation—we begin to experience our unity with the universe.

Advanced Insights into Nature, Energy, and the Human Body

1. **Microcosm and Macrocosm:** The belief that the human being is a **microcosm** of the universe is central to many spiritual systems, including the teachings of the **Siddhars** and **Kriya Yogam**. This means that everything within the body—body, mind, and spirit—is a reflection of the greater universe. The elements that make up the universe—earth, water, fire, air, and ether—are also present in our bodies. The balance of these elements is key to our health, and practices like **Kriya Yogam** and **Siddha Medicine** aim to restore that balance.
2. **Energy Flow and the Nadis:** The **Siddhars** had a profound understanding of energy flow within the body. They taught that **prana**, or life force energy, flows through channels in the body known as **nadis**. If these pathways are blocked or imbalanced, it can lead to physical or spiritual ailments. Through practices like **Pranayama** (breath control), a practitioner can clear these blockages and restore energy flow, helping to bring balance back to the body and mind.
3. **Kundalini Awakening:** At the base of the spine lies **Kundalini**, a dormant spiritual energy that, when awakened, leads to self-realization and enlightenment. In the **Siddhar** tradition, the rising of the Kundalini energy through the chakras is seen as a path to spiritual ascension. The union of **Shiva** (pure consciousness) and **Shakti** (creative energy) at the crown chakra represents the ultimate spiritual awakening. This union is known as **Samadhi** or **divine union**.

   Awakening Kundalini can bring physical, emotional, and mental benefits, including increased energy, emotional balance, and mental clarity. However, the process requires careful guidance and discipline, as it is a powerful and transformative experience.
4. **Alchemy and Transformation of the Body:** In the **Siddhar** tradition, there's a concept of **inner alchemy**, where spiritual practices refine and purify the body, mind, and soul. Just as alchemists sought to turn base metals into gold, spiritual practitioners transform

their bodies into more refined, divine forms. Through Yogam and meditation, they purify their energy and move closer to higher states of consciousness.

Some **Siddhars**, like **Mahavatar Babaji**, are believed to have achieved immortality, transcending the limits of the human body. This idea comes from the belief that when the body is in harmony with cosmic energy, it can resist decay and even heal itself from illness.

5. **The Role of Sound and Light in Spiritual Practices:** As a practitioner advances in their spiritual journey, they may experience divine **sound** and **light**. In the **Siddhar** tradition, sound is considered a powerful healing tool. **Mantras**, sacred sounds, are believed to carry divine energy and help heal the body and mind by aligning the practitioner with cosmic forces. Similarly, **inner light** is seen as a sign of spiritual awakening, illuminating the path to enlightenment.
6. **Healing Powers and Siddhis:** The **Siddhars** were also believed to possess **siddhis**, or supernatural abilities, as a result of their advanced spiritual practices. These included the ability to heal, perform miraculous feats like levitation, and even transcend the physical limitations of the human body. However, they cautioned that these powers should never be the goal of spiritual practice. Instead, the true aim is always **self-realization, liberation (moksha)**, and union with the divine.

Kriya Yogam's Connection to Siddhar Practices

While **Kriya Yogam** as we know it today is a relatively modern practice, its roots in **Siddhar** traditions are undeniable. **Mahavatar Babaji**, a central figure in the revival of Kriya Yogam, embodies the teachings of the Siddhars. His teachings highlight that Kriya Yogam is not just a technique for physical health, but a complete spiritual discipline that leads to freedom from the cycle of birth and death (samsara).

Through the practice of **Kriya Yogam**, practitioners not only achieve spiritual growth and **moksha**, but also experience practical benefits such as mental clarity, emotional stability, and improved physical health. Kriya Yogam brings practitioners into a deep connection with nature, fostering balance, healing, and a deeper understanding of their place in the cosmos.

In summary, the teachings of **Kriya Yogam** and the **Siddhar** tradition highlight that the body, mind, and spirit are deeply interconnected with the universe. By harmonizing our inner energies with cosmic forces through practices like pranayama, meditation, and Kundalini awakening, we can achieve physical well-being and spiritual enlightenment. The deeper teachings also include concepts such as mastering the elements, reversing aging, and connecting with divine forces. These practices, when followed with discipline, lead to a profound transformation, opening the path to divine wisdom and ultimate transcendence.

This chapter explores how deeply the universe, nature, and human beings are interconnected and how spiritual practices can guide us back to balance, well-being, and ultimate freedom.

BODY, MIND AND SOUL

The mind, intelligence, and ego—they each play their part in our lives. For everything to flow smoothly, the mind needs to stay calm and not jump from one thought to another. It's like having a chatty friend who can't stick to one topic! Intelligence should stay steady too—don't second-guess yourself or overthink things. Once the mind and intelligence are in sync, the ego can't mess things up. In this balanced state, everything you think and do just feels right—it's called *chitham*.

Now, *chitham* is this beautiful, peaceful state where your thoughts, feelings, and intentions are all aligned. Everything just flows without the ego getting in the way. It's like a calm, clear lake where you can see everything beneath the surface, no ripples or distractions, just a pure, peaceful state of being.

Spirituality, at its core, is realizing that nothing is fixed, nothing is separate. Everything we experience, every little thing we touch or feel, is always changing. The idea of separateness—it's an illusion. Beneath everything, there's this vast emptiness, a peaceful space where everything and nothing are one. That's the essence of spirituality—it's about realizing that deep down, there's nothing.

Now, let's talk about how we can tame the mind, something that's not easy, right? One powerful way is through *Kriya Yogam*. It's a unique type of Yogam that helps you feel more alive and at peace. When you practice Kriya, your breath slows down naturally, your heart calms, and suddenly your mind isn't bouncing around all over the place. You start to feel a deep, lasting satisfaction inside that's way beyond the usual day-to-day happiness. It's like finding a treasure that's always been there, waiting for you.

As you practice more, you begin to see the world with fresh eyes. You notice things that once flew under the radar. You feel more connected, like you're tuned into something bigger than yourself. And the best part? You start to realize that life isn't just about you—it's about something divine that connects us all.

Human life is sacred—it's not just about us, it's about aligning with the divine. That's what Kriya Yogam is all about. It's not just a practice for us as human beings—it's a way to connect us with the divine, helping us understand that the divine is within us all.

Kriya Yogam is all about balance. It involves breath control, meditation, and living with discipline to bring harmony to the body, mind, and spirit. And when you start practicing, you can raise your consciousness and feel closer to a divine state, as if you're tapping into something much greater than yourself.

The idea behind Kriya Yogam is that the divine isn't some distant thing. It's within each of us. Through Kriya Yogam, you can awaken this divine energy within you, and it's through this connection that you get closer to the ultimate goal—merging with the divine essence.

Life is often shaped by our past karma—the actions we've taken in previous lives. This karma can influence our present experiences, shaping the challenges and opportunities we face today. And if you've practiced Kriya Yogam in past lives, there's a good chance you'll feel drawn to it again in this life, picking up where you left off. It's like a spiritual continuity, a thread that connects your soul's journey across lifetimes.

Deep Kriya Yogam practice can even unlock past memories, visions, and help you see the bigger picture of your soul's journey. This awareness helps you understand how the past—your actions, choices, and spiritual practices—shapes your present life.

And as you work through past karma, Kriya Yogam helps purify your mind and soul, bringing you closer to the divine. Eventually, this journey can help you break free from the cycle of birth and rebirth, reaching a state of liberation (*moksha*), where you are in eternal peace, united with the divine.

Through Kriya Yogam, you can have profound meditative experiences. One technique is focusing on the point between your eyebrows, the *spiritual eye*. If you practice consistently, you might even see a light there. This light represents the activation of your higher consciousness, a deeper connection to universal awareness.

This experience isn't just a visual thing. It's transformational. It helps calm your mind, clear it of distractions, and open you up to a deeper, more universal state of awareness. In this state, you realize that you're not just an individual—you're part of something much bigger. This higher awareness, called *Gyanaozhi*, links your soul to the universe. It's the ultimate knowledge, the wisdom that connects you to the divine.

For anyone who's been through tough times or faced big losses, Kriya Yogam can be a lifesaver. It's a source of strength, resilience, and deep peace. It helps you navigate life's challenges with more grace and insight, guiding you through even the hardest moments.

When you practice Kriya Yogam, you also build a deeper connection with your own soul. Your soul starts talking to you, guiding you, offering clarity and wisdom. It's a dialogue that's much deeper than the everyday thoughts running through your head.

To really get the most out of Kriya Yogam, though, you need to clear out the negative emotions—things like anger and ego. These emotions can block positive energy, slow down your progress, and prevent you from growing spiritually. Let go of the anger, let go of the ego, and you'll create a clearer space for your practice to flourish.

And when it comes to material things—if someone offers you a symbol of God, or any material object—don't hold on to it too tightly. Remember, God is with you in your heart, not in physical objects. Holding onto things just creates attachment, which leads to suffering. Embrace the idea of letting go, of generosity. Trust that the divine presence is always with you, not dependent on any physical item.

By practicing detachment and giving freely, you align with the core teachings of Kriya Yogam. This fosters peace, spiritual growth, and a closer connection with the divine. True spirituality isn't about what you own; it's about what's in your heart.

As you let go of negativity, your mind becomes calmer, your focus sharpens, and you're able to meditate more deeply. This allows you to rise to higher states of consciousness and, eventually, spiritual enlightenment and liberation.

One of the most beautiful benefits of Kriya Yogam is that it keeps you feeling youthful. It harmonizes your body, mind, and spirit, making you feel at peace and vibrant from the inside out. When your inner world is aligned, it radiates outward, keeping you energized, balanced, and youthful.

Kriya Yogam reminds you that God is always with you. It's like having a constant source of strength and guidance, reassuring you that you're never alone in your spiritual journey.

Trust the process, surrender to it. Don't try to control everything. Just do your part and be happy. The universe will take care of the rest. The more you surrender, the more you'll experience the power of Kriya Yogam guiding you towards spiritual growth.

When you reach the next level of Kriya Yogam, you start to master advanced techniques like *Maha Mandiram*—a deep form of meditation that takes you further into higher states of awareness. As you meditate, you might start seeing different colors, like black, turning into blue. These colors symbolize a deeper connection to consciousness and insight.

Chanting mantras like "Om Namah Shivaya" is an important part of this practice. It helps focus your mind and connects you to the divine vibrations of Lord Shiva. And don't forget *Manam Adaganum*, which means controlling your mind. One powerful way to do this is by practicing silence—*Mouna Vratha*. Silence helps still the mind, quiet the distractions, and creates a space for deep peace.

Don't forget to do acts of charity and kindness, too. This is called *Dhana Dharma*. These acts purify your heart, help you overcome selfishness, and create positive karma, all of which support your spiritual journey.

Integrating all these practices—meditation, mantra chanting, silence, and charity—will elevate your Kriya Yogam practice, bringing you to deeper meditation and greater spiritual enlightenment.

Each day, take time to reflect on the blessings in your life, acknowledging the divine gifts you've received. Spend some quiet moments alone, maybe in a dark room with your eyes closed, and just explore your inner world. This introspection will help you understand your true self and your place in the world.

Remember, when anger flares up, it's usually because of unmet expectations. Work through these issues, and you'll find healthier relationships and emotional well-being.

The ego is sneaky—it's like sticking a needle in butter. It can slowly chip away at your humility and wisdom. Stay alert and practice humility to prevent the ego from taking over.

As we grow older, we naturally begin to accept life's impermanence. We realize how small we are in the grand scheme of things, and this brings us a sense of humility and gratitude for life's blessings.

Spiritually, it's important to remember that we live off the five elements—earth, water, fire, air, and space. They sustain us, reminding us that we're connected to everything around us.

To overcome the ego, you need to surrender with humility, focusing on service to a higher purpose. Life's accomplishments and possessions are temporary. The real fulfillment comes from living in alignment with spiritual values, serving others, and practicing compassion.

By embracing gratitude and humility, you transcend the ego's hold on your life and connect more deeply with the divine essence within you. This spiritual shift brings a profound sense of peace and fulfillment, as you begin to realize that true greatness lies not in personal achievement, but in selfless service, compassion, and spiritual growth.

Kriya Amrutham 13

Kriya Yogam acknowledges that our current life is shaped by the impressions (samskaras) and tendencies (vasanas) carried forward from previous births. These karmic imprints influence our thoughts, actions, and spiritual progress. Understanding this continuity helps explain innate talents, fears, and the challenges we face in life.

Through advanced Kriya practices, one can neutralize the effects of past karma by awakening the inner divine energy (Kundalini). This process purifies the subconscious mind, dissolving karmic debts and freeing the practitioner to live with greater clarity and purpose.

This chapter delves into how Kriya Yogam helps navigate and transcend the influences of past lives, paving the way for liberation and spiritual evolution.

Chapter 13

Previous Births Carry Forwards

An Advanced Understanding: The Carry-Forward from Previous Births

The idea that what we do in this life carries over from our past lives is not just some abstract concept. It's actually a cornerstone of many spiritual teachings, particularly in Hinduism, Buddhism, Jainism, and even in certain schools of thought like theosophy. In simple terms, it's the belief that the thoughts, actions, and desires we've accumulated from past lives shape the world we experience right now. This notion is especially relevant when you look at Kriya Yogam, yogic teachings, and the overall path of spiritual evolution. The journey of the soul, according to these traditions, is a continuous one—a path to ultimate realization. So, let's dive into this concept and explore how it all fits together.

1. Karma and Reincarnation: The Core Mechanism

The basic idea of carry-forward in spiritual teachings is built around something called the *law of karma*. This law says that everything we do—whether it's a thought, word, or action—creates consequences. These consequences can either bind us to the cycle of life and death or free us from it.

- **Binding Karma**: When we act selfishly or out of ignorance, we create attachments. These attachments pull us back into the cycle of rebirth, making us want more, desire more, and constantly chase things that can never truly satisfy us.
- **Liberating Karma**: On the other hand, when we act with love, wisdom, and a sense of service—like through meditation, selfless acts, and devotion—this kind of karma helps us break free from the cycle. It's the kind of karma that leads to liberation.

Now, when a soul moves on to a new life, it doesn't just forget what happened in the past. It brings along the mental imprints—called *samskaras*—and the karmic debts it's carried over from previous lives. This is how the soul keeps working through the unresolved issues from the past, shaping its destiny and offering new chances for growth.

2. Samskaras and Vasanas: The Mental Imprints

Imagine your mind is like a hard drive, and each experience leaves an impression on it—sometimes good, sometimes not so good. These imprints are called *samskaras*. They're the emotional responses, desires, and traumas we carry with us from one life to the next. And the *vasanas* are the subtle desires and tendencies that arise from those samskaras, which guide our actions in this life.

For someone walking the path of spiritual awakening, samskaras can either be a challenge or a tool. On the one hand, they can trap us in the same old patterns of suffering and attachment. But on the other hand, they provide the opportunity to rise above them. By working to purify them—through practices like meditation, mindfulness, and devotion—we can transcend these imprints.

- **Purification of Samskaras**: This is where practices like Kriya Yogam come into play. Through deep meditation, a practitioner can start to cleanse the mind of these old imprints. As the mind quiets, the samskaras lose their grip, making way for clearer spiritual growth.

3. The Atman (Soul) and the Individual Self (Jiva)

The *Atman* is the true, eternal self. It's the part of us that never changes, never suffers, and is untouched by the ups and downs of life. But the *jiva*—the individual soul—experiences the effects of our past lives through our connection to the body and mind. The jiva goes through cycles of birth and death until it realizes its true nature as the Atman. Once that realization happens, the soul is freed from the endless cycle of reincarnation and attains *moksha*—liberation.

- **Evolution of the Jiva**: The jiva evolves over countless lifetimes, learning from its mistakes, purifying its actions, and gradually letting go of worldly attachments. The ultimate goal is for the soul to return to its pure, unbroken state of bliss and awareness.

4. Spiritual Practices and Clearing Past Karmas

When it comes to accelerating the soul's journey, certain spiritual practices can be incredibly powerful. In the context of Kriya Yogam, meditation, pranayama (breathing techniques), and selfless service can all help clear away the karmic weight from past lives much faster than just intellectual understanding or traditional rituals.

- **Kriya Yogam and the Mind**: Kriya Yogam is one such practice that helps the practitioner access deep states of consciousness, where they can see the subtle imprints of past lives. By purifying the subconscious mind, it becomes possible to transcend the cycles of karma that come from previous births.
- **Surrender to the Divine**: Another advanced practice is surrender. It's not about passively giving up, but about trusting in the divine plan and letting go of the burden of past karma. This surrender helps to clear away the karmic weight we've carried for so long.

5. The Law of Attraction and Past Life Influences

In today's spiritual world, the idea of the *Law of Attraction* is often linked to the carry-forward concept from past lives. The basic idea of this law is that our present thoughts and actions shape our future. But when you add in the influence of past lives, it becomes clear that our past desires, emotions, and unfinished business from previous births often play a huge role in what we encounter today.

- **Synchronicity and Past Life Connections**: Ever had a random encounter with someone, and it just felt like you knew them? Well, according to advanced teachings, this could be a karmic connection from a past life. People who cross our path might have been part of our lives before, and unresolved karma can bring them back to us for a reason.

6. Soul Groups and Karmic Relationships

There's also the concept of *soul groups*. These are groups of souls that have shared past experiences and come together in future lifetimes to resolve unfinished business. Have you ever met someone and just felt an instant connection, like you've known them forever? That could be a sign of a karmic relationship. These relationships carry forward from past lives, giving us opportunities for growth, healing, and transformation.

7. Advanced Techniques for Accelerating Liberation

When it comes to accelerating liberation, there are advanced techniques that focus on dissolving past karmas. The practice becomes about consciously letting go of the old patterns that keep us stuck and realizing our true nature.

- **Kundalini Awakening**: Kundalini energy, when it rises through the chakras, can purify the body and mind, helping to dissolve the karmic residues from previous lives.
- **Transcending the Ego**: Ultimately, the key to breaking free from the cycle of karma is transcending the ego. When we realize that we are one with the Divine, and that everything in existence is non-dual, we no longer have to be weighed down by the past. The soul is then free to return to its original state of pure consciousness.

Lord Krishna's Teachings on Previous Births in the Bhagavad Gita

In the *Bhagavad Gita*, Lord Krishna touches on the idea of past lives and their impact on the soul's journey. He explains that the soul is eternal and that it continues its evolution through multiple lifetimes. Krishna's teachings also show that by understanding our past lives, we can understand our true divine nature and purpose.

- **Bhagavad Gita, Chapter 4, Verse 5**: Krishna says that even though his physical body may appear to die, the soul never does. Just as Krishna incarnates in different forms to help guide humanity, the soul too continues its journey through multiple lifetimes.
- **Bhagavad Gita, Chapter 2, Verse 12**: Krishna says that there was never a time when the soul didn't exist, and there will never be a time when it ceases to exist. This reinforces the idea that the soul's journey is timeless, with the influence of past actions carried forward.
- **Bhagavad Gita, Chapter 9, Verse 22**: Krishna reassures us that if we remain devoted and focused on the Divine, we can overcome past karmas. By doing so, we draw closer to our true nature and neutralize the karmic effects from previous births.

Breaking the Cycle of Rebirth

Krishna also teaches that through devotion, meditation, and selfless action, the soul can transcend the carry-forward of previous lives. When we let go of our attachment to the material world, surrender to the Divine, and recognize our eternal nature as the Atman, the cycle of rebirth no longer holds power over us. The ultimate goal is moksha—liberation from the endless cycles of birth and death.

Through grace, the soul can finally reunite with the Divine and return to its original, undivided state of bliss and awareness. At that point, the influence of past lives fades away, and the soul is free to experience the true peace of its divine nature.

In summary, the concept of carrying forward from previous births is an essential part of the soul's evolutionary journey. By understanding how past karma and mental imprints influence our present lives, and by using advanced spiritual practices to purify ourselves, we can accelerate our path to liberation. The teachings of Lord Krishna in the *Bhagavad Gita* offer profound insights on how to break free from the limitations of past births and move toward our ultimate realization.

Karma Siddhanta (the law of karma), illustrating the balance of actions and consequences

Kriya Amrutham 14

The Human Body: An Unimaginable Creation

The human body is a marvel of divine intelligence, intricately designed as a vessel for spiritual awakening. In Kriya Yogam, it is seen as a microcosm of the universe, with energy centers (chakras), pathways (nadis), and the dormant Kundalini Shakti forming a perfect system for inner transformation.

Advanced teachings reveal that the body is not merely physical but also a subtle and causal system that bridges the material and spiritual realms. By activating and aligning these dimensions through Kriya practices, one unlocks hidden potentials, including heightened awareness, vitality, and spiritual realization.

This chapter explores the divine architecture of the human form, emphasizing its role as a sacred tool for self-discovery and unity with the cosmos.

Chapter 14

The Human Body: An Unimaginable Creation

The Human Body and the Path to Spiritual Awakening

The human body, in its intricate biological design and profound spiritual significance, stands as a powerful symbol of the soul's journey through the material world. It is not merely a biological organism but a temple for the divine presence, a vehicle for the soul's evolution, and an instrument for attaining self-realization. Ancient scriptures, spiritual texts, and modern scientific understanding offer varying perspectives on the body's mysteries, but in spiritual traditions, it is viewed as the medium through which the soul interacts with the material world and advances toward ultimate liberation.

1. The Human Body: A Divine Instrument

From a spiritual standpoint, the human body is a sacred instrument through which the soul (Atman) experiences life. According to Vedic and Yogic teachings, the body is not merely flesh and bones but a vessel created by divine intelligence, reflecting the cosmos itself. It is through this sacred vessel that the soul undergoes the process of evolution, seeking self-realization, inner peace, and ultimately union with the Divine.

The Subtle and Gross Bodies

- **The Gross Body (Sthula Sharira)**: This is the physical body, composed of the five elements: earth, water, fire, air, and ether. While it is governed by biological laws, from a spiritual perspective, it is just a temporary vehicle for the soul's experiences.

- **The Subtle Body (Sukshma Sharira)**: This body encompasses the mind, intellect, emotions, and ego, and carries the accumulated karma and tendencies from previous lifetimes (samskaras and vasanas). It influences one's actions, desires, and spiritual growth.
- **The Causal Body (Karana Sharira)**: The deepest layer of existence, the causal body holds the seeds of karma, latent desires, and potentialities. It is from here that the other two bodies emerge, and through spiritual practices, it can be transcended when the soul attains moksha (liberation).

These three bodies work in harmony, providing the framework for the soul's journey through multiple lifetimes. The purification and transcendence of these bodies are central to spiritual evolution.

2. The Body as a Microcosm of the Universe

The human body is often described as a microcosm—a miniature reflection of the macrocosm of the universe. This concept finds expression in ancient yogic scriptures, such as the Yogam Sutras of Patanjali, which describe the body as a vessel for prana (life force) that flows through it in channels called **nadis**. The **chakras**, or energy centers, are the focal points of this prana, governing the body's spiritual, mental, and physical well-being.

The **seven primary chakras** (Muladhara, Svadhishthana, Manipura, Anahata, Vishuddha, Ajna, Sahasrara) are energy centers that correspond to various aspects of existence. The awakening and balancing of these chakras allow the soul to ascend in consciousness, ultimately leading to higher states of spiritual awareness and union with the Divine.

3. The Five Koshas (Sheaths) and Their Functions

The concept of the **five koshas** (sheaths) offers a deeper understanding of the layers of consciousness that reside within the human body. Each kosha represents a different aspect of being, from the physical to the transcendent:

1. **Annamaya Kosha**: The physical body, made of food (anna), is the outermost layer.
2. **Pranamaya Kosha**: The energy body, which consists of prana, the life force that sustains the body and mind.
3. **Manomaya Kosha**: The mental body, responsible for thoughts, emotions, and desires.
4. **Vijnanamaya Kosha**: The wisdom body, related to higher intellect, discernment, and spiritual insight.
5. **Anandamaya Kosha**: The bliss body, the innermost sheath, where pure bliss and spiritual ecstasy reside.

As one progresses spiritually, they move inward through these koshas, transcending the physical to experience deeper states of awareness. This progression represents the purification of the body, mind, and soul.

4. The Mystery of Consciousness

Consciousness is the fundamental nature of the soul (Atman), according to Vedanta and yogic philosophy. While the body and mind act as instruments for experiencing and perceiving the world, consciousness itself remains unchanging and eternal. The mind, with its thoughts and impressions, is an intermediary through which consciousness perceives reality. However, when the mind is stilled through deep meditation or self-inquiry (Atma Vichara), the soul recognizes its true, unchanging nature, transcending the limitations of the physical body.

5. The Body's Role in Spiritual Evolution

The body is not merely a vessel of material existence but also the vehicle for spiritual evolution. According to yogic teachings, attaining self-realization requires the purification of the body, mind, and spirit:

- **The Physical Body**: Through **Yogam asanas** (postures), **pranayama** (breath control), and detoxification, the physical body becomes a clear and receptive instrument for the flow of divine energy.
- **The Subtle Body**: Through practices like **meditation, mantra chanting**, and **contemplation**, the mind is purified, releasing attachments and distractions, which allows the practitioner to gain spiritual clarity.
- **The Causal Body**: The deepest spiritual practices, such as intense meditation and devotion, work to dissolve the latent desires and karmic patterns stored in the causal body, ultimately allowing the soul to transcend the cycle of birth and death (samsara).

6. Insights from Ancient Scriptures

Ancient scriptures, from the **Upanishads** to the **Bhagavad Gita**, offer profound insights into the connection between the body, soul, and the universe.

- **Upanishads**: The body is described as the temple of the soul, where the soul undergoes experiences to realize its oneness with the Divine. The **Chandogya Upanishad** speaks of the body as a microcosm of the universe, while the **Mundaka Upanishad** highlights the body as a vehicle for realizing the ultimate truth (Brahman).

  Chandogya Upanishad 3.14.1:
  "The body is the temple of the soul. It is through this temple that the soul experiences the world and is meant to realize its oneness with the divine."

- **Bhagavad Gita**: Lord Krishna discusses the impermanence of the body and the immortality of the soul. He emphasizes that the soul is eternal, unaffected by birth and death, while the body is a temporary vessel.

Bhagavad Gita, Chapter 2, Verse 13:

"Just as the boyhood, youth, and old age come to the embodied soul in this body, in the same manner, old age comes to the soul in another body. The wise man is not deluded at that."

Bhagavad Gita, Chapter 2, Verse 20:

"For the soul, there is neither birth nor death at any time. It is not slain when the body is slain."

- **Tantra and Yogic Philosophy**: The **Tantras** and **Yogam Sutras of Patanjali** offer detailed descriptions of the body's energetic system, including the flow of prana through the nadis and chakras. These texts teach that the body is sacred, and through spiritual practices, one can awaken the dormant energy (Kundalini) and achieve spiritual enlightenment.

7. The Body: A Unification of Spirit and Matter

The human body represents the union of the material and spiritual realms. It is a physical entity made of the same elements as the universe, yet it serves as the medium through which the infinite consciousness of the soul expresses itself. This union—the intersection of finite and infinite—forms the mystery of life itself. Through dedicated spiritual practice, the individual can awaken to the realization that they are not merely the body but the eternal consciousness within.

Conclusion

The human body, in its biological and metaphysical dimensions, is an extraordinary creation. It is both a physical vessel for the soul's experiences and a spiritual instrument for the soul's evolution. Through understanding and spiritual practice, the body can become a powerful tool for attaining liberation (moksha), self-realization, and union with the Divine. The body is not merely a temporary existence; it is a sacred temple in which the soul seeks to realize its ultimate truth and divine essence.

Kriya Amrutham 15

Kriya Yogam for every one

"A little knowledge of science makes you an atheist, in depth knowledge of science makes you a believer in God"

– Louis Pasteur
Founder of Microbiology and Immunology

Chapter 15

Polluted Cells, Ailments and Aging

How Oxygen and Prana Affect Health and Wellness

1. **Oxygen Levels and Health**

   - **Oxygen's Role:** Oxygen is crucial for cell function, energy production, and detoxification. Low oxygen levels (hypoxia) can disrupt cell health, leading to oxidative stress, inflammation, and damage. These effects are linked to chronic conditions like heart disease, diabetes, and neurological disorders.
   - **Health Impacts of Low Oxygen:** Poor oxygen levels are associated with fatigue, cognitive decline, weakened immunity, and organ dysfunction. Hypoxia also correlates with conditions such as hypertension, sleep apnea, stroke, and heart disease(1)

2. **Prana (Vital Life Energy) and Health in Yogic Terms**

   - **Role of Prana:** Prana, or life force, sustains mental and physical health. It flows through energy channels (nadis), with key centers (chakras) along the spine regulating bodily functions. Disrupted Prana flow may result in physical ailments, stress, and reduced immunity. Practices like Kriya Yogam, Pranayama, and meditation help restore Prana flow, enhancing vitality and well-being(2,3).
   - **Health Impact of Prana Depletion:** Reduced Prana can lead to fatigue, mental stress, and, if persistent, chronic illness. Studies on breath-based practices indicate improvements in stress reduction, autonomic function, and respiratory health, promoting both mental and physical well-being(2).

3. The Link Between Prana and Oxygen

While oxygen is a physical necessity, Prana is a subtle energy in yogic philosophy. They're interconnected, as breathing exercise like Pranayama increases oxygen and Prana simultaneously. Oxygen supports physical health, while Prana helps maintain a balance between mental well-being and energy(4).

Revitalization and Anti-Aging Effects of Oxygen and Prana

1. Enhanced Oxygen Intake and Cellular Health

- **Oxygen's Role in Cellular Regeneration:** Oxygen supports cellular energy production. Controlled breathing (e.g., Pranayama) enhances lung function, circulation, and mental health, benefiting cell health. Oxygen-rich environments are also known to support cellular repair and regeneration.
- **Hyperbaric Oxygen Therapy (HBOT):** HBOT increases blood oxygen levels, promoting healing, reducing inflammation, and potentially slowing cellular ageing by stimulating stem cells and reducing oxidative stress(5,6).

2. Prana and Vitality from a Yogic Perspective

- **Prana as Life Force:** Prana sustains physical, mental, and spiritual health. Breath-focused practices, such as Pranayama in Kriya Yogam, are believed to increase vitality, reduce ailments, and calm the mind. When Prana flows freely, it revitalizes the body and enhances immunity.
- **Benefits of Controlled Breathing:** Breathing techniques, particularly those that slow and control the breath, activate the parasympathetic nervous system, reducing stress and promoting healing. Studies show that controlled breathing exercise lowers blood pressure, improves heart rate variability, and reduces inflammation, all essential for cellular health and longevity.

3. Anti-Ageing and Disease Prevention Potential

- **Reducing Oxidative Stress:** Oxidative stress, associated with chronic diseases, damages cells through the action of free radicals. Breathing exercises and oxygenation practices can reduce oxidative stress, contributing to an anti-aging effect. Research indicates that long-term practitioners of Yogam and meditation have lower inflammation markers, suggesting benefits for longevity..
- **Strengthening Immunity:** Increasing oxygen and Prana through breathing exercisemay strengthen immunity, making the body more resilient. Practices like Kriya Yogam show improvements in immune response, stress reduction, and balanced hormonal levels.

Conclusion

While breathing techniques and oxygen therapies don't halt ageing, they support cellular health, boost immunity, reduce inflammation, and enhance mental well-being. These combined effects may slow ageing and reduce the likelihood of chronic diseases, through lifestyle and diet modifications also play critical roles in long-term health.

Longevity and Rejuvenation in Yogic Tradition

The belief that advanced yogis, especially those in remote Himalayan regions, can live for extraordinarily long periods—sometimes even hundreds of years—originates from yogic philosophy and accounts of practitioners who have reached a profound mastery over their body and mind. Stories suggest that these yogis achieve mastery over Prana (vital life force), meditation, and various other yogic practices, which may rejuvenate the body, enhance health, and possibly extend lifespan. However, scientific verification of lifespans extending into centuries remains anecdotal, with limited empirical evidence to support these claims..

How Rejuvenation Could Extend Longevity in Yogic Practice

1. **Prana Control and Cellular Health:** Advanced Prana control in yogic practices, like Kriya Yogam and Pranayama (breath control), is thought to impact the body's life force directly. This continuous Prana flow, in yogic belief, helps reduce oxidative stress and promotes cellular repair, rejuvenating the organs, strengthening immunity, and slowing the bodily ageing. Some practitioners believe these effects lead to noticeable anti-ageing and resistance to illness.
2. **Adaptation to High Altitude and Reduced Oxygen Needs:** Himalayan yogis often live at high altitudes with low oxygen levels, adapting their bodies to function with minimal oxygen. Yogic practices that involve slow breathing, like deep meditation, are said to train the body to minimize oxygen needs, reduce metabolic stress, and potentially increase lifespan. Scientific studies on high-altitude adaptations support that these environments can enhance oxygen efficiency, which may positively impact health and ageing.
3. **Meditation and Telomere Length:** Telomeres are protective caps on chromosomes that shorten with age, contributing to cellular ageing. Research has shown that regular meditation can slow telomere shortening, suggesting a cellular-level impact on ageing. However, while promising, these results indicate only modest lifespan extension, rather than the extreme longevity sometimes attributed to Himalayan yogis(7,8).
4. **Immune and Hormonal Regulation:** Long-term Yogam and meditation practitioners tend to have lower levels of stress hormones like cortisol, as well as greater resistance to inflammation. Reduced chronic inflammation is essential for healthy ageing since inflammation contributes to many age-related diseases. These effects may enhance resilience to illness and promote longer healthier lives.

5. **Anecdotal Accounts and Traditional Claims:** Stories of Himalayan yogis who have reportedly lived far beyond a normal lifespan are found within spiritual traditions, with figures like Mahavatar Babaji said to have reached a "deathless" state through advanced Kriya practices. Although these accounts lack scientific corroboration, they emphasize the potential of yogic mastery to extend life, possibly beyond ordinary limits.

Scientific Perspective

While yoga, meditation, and breathing exercise have shown clear benefits for health, including disease resilience and improved quality of life, their ability to extend life by hundreds of years remains unverified scientifically. Current evidence points to enhanced wellness and longevity within normal biological limits rather than extreme life extension.

Kriya Yogam, Pranayama, and Meditation for Chronic Disease Management

Engaging in regular practice of Kriya Yogam, Pranayama, and meditation, which emphasize enhancing oxygen and Prana flow, has demonstrated potential for alleviating symptoms and possibly reversing some effects of chronic diseases. Here is an overview of how these practices can benefit various conditions.:

1. **Cardiovascular Diseases**

   - **How It Helps:** Breath control and meditation help regulate blood pressure, improve heart rate variability, and reduce heart disease risk by lowering stress hormones and inflammation.
   - **Evidence:** Studies have shown that practices like Kriya Yogam can reduce hypertension, improve lipid profiles, and decrease stress, all contributing to better heart health.

2. **Diabetes (Type 2)**
   - **How It Helps:** Yoga practices such as cleansing processes, asanas, pranayama, mudras, bandha, meditation, mindfulness, and relaxation are known to reduce blood glucose levels and to help in the management of comorbid disease conditions associated with type 2 diabetes mellitus, resulting in significant positive clinical outcomes.
   - **Evidence:** Research indicates that regular Pranayama and meditation practice can reduce fasting blood glucose levels and improve glycemic control in type 2 diabetes patients.
3. **Respiratory Disorders (e.g., Asthma, COPD)**
   - **How It Helps:** Pranayama enhances lung capacity, strengthens respiratory muscles, and promotes efficient oxygen use. For asthma and COPD, specific breathing techniques improve lung function and calm airway inflammation.
   - **Evidence:** Clinical studies on Yogam and Pranayama show improved respiratory function, reduced asthma attack frequency, and enhanced breathing efficiency in COPD patients.
4. **Chronic Pain and Arthritis**
   - **How It Helps:** Yogam and meditation help alleviate pain and improve joint function by increasing endorphin release and reducing inflammation, particularly beneficial for arthritis and chronic pain.
   - **Evidence:** Studies have shown that Yogam and breathing exercise significantly reduce pain in arthritis and chronic pain patients, increasing mobility and comfort.
5. **Anxiety, Depression, and Mental Health Disorders**
   - **How It Helps:** Techniques to increase Prana flow and oxygenation balance the neurotransmitters and reduce stress hormones, promoting mental clarity, anxiety reduction, and mood stabilization.

- **Evidence:** Research in psychoneuroimmunology shows that meditation and breath control reduce anxiety and depression symptoms by lowering cortisol and balancing serotonin and dopamine levels.

6. **Autoimmune Disorders**
   - **How It Helps:** Chronic inflammation plays a major role in autoimmune diseases. Yogam and Pranayama help regulate immune responses and reduce inflammation, aiding in managing conditions like lupus erythematous, rheumatoid arthritis, and multiple sclerosis.
   - **Evidence:** Studies show that meditation and breathing exercise modulate immune function and reduce inflammatory markers, benefiting autoimmune patients.

7. **Digestive Disorders (e.g., IBS, GERD)**
   - **How It Helps:** Yogic practices calm the nervous system, enhancing digestive efficiency and reducing IBS and GERD symptoms. Breathing exercise helps minimize stress responses, which are often linked to digestive issues.
   - **Evidence:** Controlled trials indicate that Yogam reduces IBS symptoms and improves digestion in those with chronic digestive disorders.

8. **Cancer Support and Recovery**
   - **How It Helps:** While not a cure, Yogam and breathing exercise can help reduce side effects, improve immune function, and enhance well-being during cancer therapy.
   - **Evidence:** Research shows Yogam and meditation improve quality of life, reduce fatigue, and may aid immune recovery in cancer patients, making them valuable supportive therapies.

These findings suggest that practices like Kriya Yogam, Pranayama, and meditation can support conventional treatments and play a powerful role in holistic health, especially when integrated consistently.

Additional Insights into Yogic Practices for Long-Term Health and Healing

The benefits of yoga, breathing exercise, and meditation extend beyond symptom relief and stress reduction, influencing deeper levels of healing, resilience, and physical rejuvenation. Here are some additional perspectives to enrich our understanding of these practices:

1. **Holistic Cellular Rejuvenation**
   - **Impact on Cellular Health:** Regular breathing exercise and meditative practices stimulate oxygenation at a cellular level, supporting mitochondrial function, which is essential for energy production and cellular repair. Consistent oxygen intake through Pranayama can help decrease oxidative stress and promote healthier cell turnover, which is vital for long-term rejuvenation and resilience.
   - **Influence on Stem Cells and Regeneration:** Although this area is still being explored, early studies suggest that mindful breathing and meditative states may influence stem cell activity, potentially enhancing the body's natural regenerative processes.
2. **Enhanced Autonomic Nervous System Regulation**
   - **Balance Between Sympathetic and Parasympathetic Systems:** Yogam and meditation activate the parasympathetic nervous system (the "rest and digest" state), which balances out the sympathetic system (the "fight or flight" state). This balance is crucial for those with chronic conditions, as it lowers the levels of stress hormones, reduces inflammation, and helps the body conserve energy for healing.
   - **Improved Heart Rate Variability (HRV):** Higher HRV, a measure of autonomic nervous system resilience, is associated with better health and longevity. Practices that enhance HRV, such as slow breathing and meditation, may improve resilience and the body's adaptability to stress, which can be especially beneficial for chronic disease management.

3. **Supporting Endocrine Health**
   - **Hormonal Balance Through Breath and Postures:** Specific Yogam postures and breathing techniques influence glands in the endocrine system, helping regulate hormones, which play a critical role in stress management, metabolism, and immunity. For instance, adrenal and thyroid health is often supported by deep, steady breathing and postures that gently stretch the neck area, potentially benefiting metabolic health and energy balance.
   - **Reduction of Inflammatory Markers:** Chronic diseases often coincide with elevated inflammation. Yogic practices, which activate the parasympathetic response, are shown to lower levels of pro-inflammatory cytokines, reducing stress-induced inflammation that can accelerate disease progression.
4. **Emotional and Mental Resilience**
   - **Stress and Emotional Healing:** Chronic illnesses can be emotionally challenging. Yogam and meditation not only reduce physiological stress but also foster mental resilience, offering tools for managing the emotional aspects of long-term health conditions. They help cultivate patience, self-acceptance, and a deeper connection to one's inner self, which can lead to a more positive outlook and greater resilience to life's challenges.
   - **Brain Plasticity and Cognitive Health:** Meditation and mindfulness practices enhance brain plasticity, improving memory, concentration, and emotional regulation. This mental flexibility is key to managing complex health conditions, as it enhances cognitive health and helps practitioners remain adaptable and centered.
5. **Prana and the Energy Body in Healing**
   - **Subtle Energy Flow and Disease Prevention:** In yogic philosophy, maintaining a balanced Prana flow throughout the body's nadis

(energy channels) prevents energy blockages, which are believed to be at the root of physical and mental ailments. Practices like Kriya Yogam and Pranayama focus on clearing these channels to prevent disease and promote vitality.

- **Conscious Control Over Prana for Healing:** Advanced practitioners learn to direct Prana consciously to areas in need of healing, such as the heart, liver, or kidneys. Although anecdotal, yogis report that directing Prana improves vitality in affected organs, leading to faster recovery and overall energy renewal.

Summary

In summary, regular practice of yoga, pranayama, and meditation promotes holistic well-being and enhances both physiological and energetic resilience, supporting long-term healing. While these practices are not substitutes for conventional treatments, they effectively reduce stress, inflammation, and improve cellular health and emotional resilience, making them valuable allies in the pursuit of better health. When integrated alongside medical care, these practices contribute to a comprehensive approach to managing chronic diseases, improving quality of life, and supporting longevity and rejuvenation.

Incorporating these practices and mindful living into daily routines not only aids in managing chronic diseases and recovering from addiction but also fosters overall well-being, resilience, and longevity. Here's a consolidated overview of the various benefits these practices offer:

1. **Holistic Impact on the Endocrine System**
   - *Hormone Balance and Stress Reduction:* Yogic techniques, especially Pranayama (such as Nadi Shodhana), balance the nervous and endocrine systems, regulating hormones that control stress, metabolism, and immune response. This contributes to mental clarity, emotional stability, and better immunity.

2. **Longevity and Cellular Health**

    - *Telomerase Activation and Anti-Aging Effects:* Research on meditation indicates it may promote telomerase activity, supporting telomere health and longevity. This cellular-level anti-ageing effect is crucial for resilience against disease and maintaining youthful energy.

3. **Mental Resilience in Chronic Illness**

    - *Emotional Support and Stress Management:* Yogam and meditation provide mental resilience, helping individuals with chronic conditions manage anxiety and depression. Practices like mindfulness meditation, Yogam nidra, and Sudarshan Kriya help regulate mood, reducing the burden of chronic stress on physical health.

4. **Energy Flow and Prana Management (Nadis and Chakras)**

    - *Esoteric Aspects of Healing:* Advanced practices, such as Kriya Yogam and Kundalini, cultivate Prana flow through the body's energy channels (Nadis) and chakras, believed to promote health, emotional balance, and spiritual growth. These techniques support a holistic healing approach, emphasizing the mind-body-spirit connection.

5. **Yogic Diet and Detoxification**

    - *Sattvic Diet for Detox and Inflammation Reduction:* Traditional yogic diets focus on plant-based, unprocessed foods that foster Prana and reduce disease risk. Fasting and cleansing routines support digestive health, giving the body time to detox and rejuvenate, aiding in overall vitality.

6. **Immunomodulation and Inflammatory Response**

    - *Balanced Immune System:* Pranayama and Yogam may balance immune responses, helping manage autoimmune conditions and reducing chronic inflammation. This enhances the body's ability to fend off illness without overstimulating immune responses, promoting long-term health.

7. **Addiction Recovery and Detoxification**

   - *Detox Support and Habit Formation:* Yoga, breathing exercise, and meditation help ease withdrawal symptoms, manage stress, and clear the body of toxins. Practices like Kapalabhati and Bhastrika aid lung and liver detox, while mindfulness retrains the brain's habit loops, supporting recovery and reducing the likelihood of relapse.

8. **Sound Mind and Body Interconnection**

   - *Physical Health's Role in Mental Well-Being:* Physical health improves circulation and neurotransmitter balance and lowers inflammation, all of which enhance cognitive function, mood stability, and mental resilience. Mind-body practices like Yogam not only reduce stress but promote neurogenesis and emotional equilibrium, reinforcing a sound mind-body connection.

9. **Building a Supportive Routine and Community**

   - *Accountability and Social Connection:* Regular Yogam and meditation foster self-discipline and provide a structured routine. Engaging in group sessions offers social support and a shared healing environment, essential for managing stress and addiction recovery.

10. **Integration with Professional Medical Support**

    - *Complementary, Not Substitute for Medical Care:* Yoga, Pranayama, and meditation serve as complementary practices, enhancing the effects of medical treatments by promoting relaxation, improving immune function, and alleviating symptoms. However, they should be integrated with professional medical care, especially for those with chronic or severe conditions.

In summary, adopting a holistic lifestyle that combines yogic practices, mindful living, balanced nutrition, and physical exercise creates a foundation for long-lasting health and resilience. By addressing body, mind, and spirit, this approach allows individuals to cultivate a life of vitality, emotional balance, and spiritual growth, making it an invaluable path for anyone seeking deeper healing and well-being.

Research article references.

1. Turnbull CD. Intermittent hypoxia, cardiovascular disease and obstructive sleep apnoea. J Thorac Dis. 2018 Jan;10(Suppl 1):S33–9.
2. Sheikh S, Rostami A, Shahbazi A, Abdollahi Nezhad F, Khazai O, Arbabisarjou A. Clinical effectiveness of guided breathing exercises in reducing anxiety, stress, and depression in COVID-19 patients. Sci Rep. 2024 Nov 4;14(1):26620.
3. Mondal S. Proposed physiological mechanisms of pranayama: A discussion. J Ayurveda Integr Med. 2024;15(1):100877.
4. Srinivasan T. Prana and electrons in health and beyond. Int J Yoga. 2014;7(1):1–3.

5. Fu Q, Duan R, Sun Y, Li Q. Hyperbaric oxygen therapy for healthy aging: From mechanisms to therapeutics. Redox Biol. 2022 May 27;53:102352.

6. Gupta M, Rathored J. Hyperbaric oxygen therapy: future prospects in regenerative therapy and anti-aging. Front Aging. 2024 May 2;5:1368982.

7. Conklin QA, King BG, Zanesco AP, Lin J, Hamidi AB, Pokorny JJ, et al. Insight meditation and telomere biology: The effects of intensive retreat and the moderating role of personality. Brain Behav Immun. 2018 May 1;70:233–45.

8. Schutte NS, Malouff JM, Keng SL. Meditation and telomere length: a meta-analysis. Psychol Health. 2020 Aug;35(8):901–15.

9. Raveendran AV, Deshpandae A, Joshi SR. Therapeutic Role of Yogam in Type 2 Diabetes. Endocrinol Metab. 2018 Sep;33(3):307–17.

Kriya Amrutham 16

Practicing Kriya

with your

loved ones creates a

special bond

that keeps the

family connected,

ensuring a sense of

unity and

understanding among

all family members.

Chapter 16

Healthy Body and A Sound Mind

Living a Happy Life with Spiritual Support

Key Aspects to Embrace:

1. **Mercy and Compassion:**
   - Even the most enlightened beings need mercy in their hearts to attain their highest spiritual goals. Without compassion, they must return to cultivate it in another life.
   - True enlightenment requires "Annbu" (love), "Karunai" (compassion), and "Jeeva Karunyam" (compassion for all living beings). These qualities are essential in your spiritual journey.
2. **Love and Care for Family:**
   - Speak to your family with love and care, as every word can be a blessing.
   - Small acts of kindness—whether through words, actions, or financial help—will return to you multiplied. Showing love to those closest to you is both a spiritual and practical way to create harmony.
3. **Understanding Human Potential:**
   - Humans have boundless potential but often fail to realize it. We try to control everything around us, forgetting that we are part of nature, not separate from it.
   - Think of yourself as a drop of water in the ocean. When you align with nature's flow, everything moves smoothly and safely. Let go of the need to control and allow yourself to flow with the current.

4. **Acceptance and Enlightenment:**
   - Accepting your ignorance is a fundamental step toward enlightenment. Like Gautama Buddha, acknowledging the limits of your knowledge opens you to deeper understanding and spiritual growth.
   - True wisdom begins with humility—understanding that there is always more to learn and experience.

5. **Letting Go:**
   - Those who are willing to let go of everything will gain everything. This is a core principle of nature.
   - Chasing material desires often leads to ill health and dissatisfaction. True peace comes from detachment and embracing the flow of life without getting caught in worldly pursuits.

6. **Living on Earth, Not Inside It:**
   - Many people mistakenly believe they live inside the earth. In reality, we live on it, surrounded by distractions.
   - These distractions can pull you away from your spiritual path, so it's important to remain grounded in the present moment and focused on your ultimate goal of liberation ("Mukthi").

7. **Karma and Liberation:**
   - The actions you take, or *karma*, come back to you. The key to liberation is to act with pure intention, avoiding the extremes of good and bad actions. As Adi Shankaracharya said, "Na punyam Na paapam"—neither good nor bad.
   - Remember, the body and its experiences are part of a larger cycle of birth and death. Seeking transient pleasures only leads to pain, addiction, and distraction from your true purpose.

8. **Mind Control and Self-Realization:**

    - Understanding and controlling your mind is a key aspect of success. Focus on the lessons you've learned, and make them a daily practice.
    - Dwelling on pain only brings more pain. Practices like meditation and *Diksha* (initiation) can provide the inner strength and peace you need to transcend suffering.

9. **Repentance and Divine Forgiveness:**

    - Repent for past actions through self-realization and seeking forgiveness from the Divine. True repentance brings divine blessings and purifies your soul.
    - When you sincerely repent and seek to realign with your higher purpose, God's grace will flow toward you.

10. **Following Universal Laws:**

    - Aligning your life with the universal laws ensures spiritual growth. These laws are the natural rhythms of the universe, guiding you toward peace and harmony.
    - Avoid rigid expectations about your spiritual journey. Instead, focus on applying the principles of your practice and remaining in harmony with nature's flow.

11. **Respecting the Guru:**

    - The guru is a living embodiment of spiritual wisdom. Respect your guru not just for their physical form, but for their spiritual role in your life.
    - The guru is not separate from you—they walk the path alongside you, and their teachings guide you toward deeper knowledge. If you have challenges with your spiritual practice, turn to your guru for guidance.

12. Continuous Practice:

- Discontinuing your spiritual practice is unfortunate, as it may require you to resume the journey in another life.
- You are fortunate to have taken birth as a human, even more so to begin contemplating the spiritual path. And, through Kriya Yogam, you are blessed with the opportunity to connect directly with the Divine.

13. Individual Experiences and Karma:

- Spiritual experiences differ based on individual karma. Following the guidance of your guru and adhering to ethical principles like Yama and Niyama is essential for progress.
- Disrespecting these principles can distance you from spiritual growth and delay your journey.

14. Fear and Karma Cleansing:

- Fear is a natural response during intense spiritual practice. Shortness of breath or physical discomfort are signs that your accumulated karma is being cleansed, leading to spiritual purification.
- Understand that this fear and discomfort are part of the process of releasing old karmas and evolving toward a higher state of being.

Key Practices to Cultivate:

- **Daily Acts of Kindness:** Make it a habit to show love and care for others through small, everyday gestures.
- **Acceptance and Letting Go:** Embrace your limitations and surrender desires to find peace and freedom.
- **Mind Control:** Use meditation and self-discipline to master your mind and its impulses.

- **Follow Spiritual Guidance:** Respect your guru's teachings and stay aligned with their wisdom.
- **Continuous Practice:** Keep your spiritual practice consistent. This is the key to connecting with the divine and achieving inner growth.

By integrating these practices into your life, you can live a life filled with happiness, peace, and spiritual fulfillment. The path to liberation may not always be easy, but it is one of great reward, offering you a deep connection with yourself, others, and the Divine.

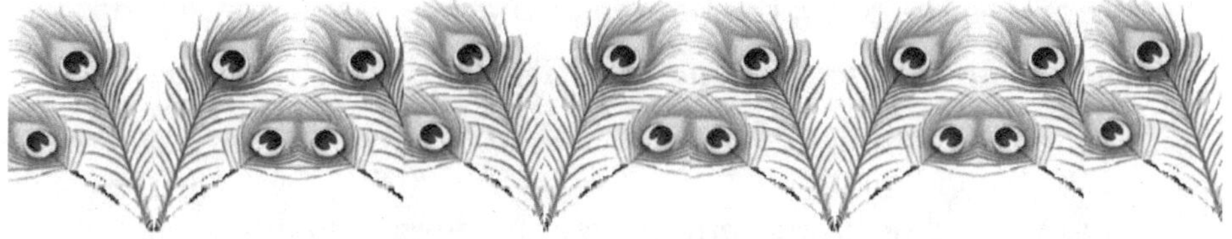

Kriya Amrutham 17

Eat Food as Medicine

In Kriya Yogam, food is not merely sustenance but a sacred offering to the body, the temple of the soul. Consuming food with awareness and balance purifies the body, sharpens the mind, and elevates spiritual energy.

Advanced teachings emphasize the gunas (qualities) of food—sattvic (pure), rajasic (stimulating), and tamasic (dulling)—and their impact on consciousness. A diet rich in sattvic foods like fresh fruits, vegetables, nuts, and grains enhances energy flow, aids meditation, and harmonizes the Pancha Bhutas within.

Kriya practitioners also consider the subtle vibrations of food, believing that meals prepared with love and consumed mindfully carry higher pranic energy. This chapter explores how treating food as medicine not only heals the body but also nurtures the soul, fostering a deep connection between nourishment and spiritual growth.

Chapter 17

Eat Food as Medicine

Food as Medicine for Kriya Yogam Practitioners

A mindful, nourishing diet plays a crucial role in supporting the body and mind on the spiritual path of Kriya Yogam. Given that Kriya Yogam involves deep meditation, intense focus, and subtle energy work, the right foods can enhance one's practice by promoting vitality, mental clarity, and spiritual alignment.

The Importance of Food as Medicine in Kriya Yogam

1. **Energy and Vitality:**
   - The goal is to consume foods that provide sustained energy without causing overstimulation or fatigue. A Kriya Yogi's diet should support natural vitality while preventing digestive strain or lethargy.
2. **Sattvic Quality:**
   - Maintaining a sattvic (pure, balanced, and harmonious) state of mind is vital for deep meditation and energy work. Sattvic foods—fresh, light, and nutrient-dense—support the flow of prana (life force) and enhance meditation and breath control.
3. **Balancing Doshas:**
   - According to Ayurveda, each person has a unique constitution (dosha—Vata, Pitta, or Kapha). A diet that balances one's dominant dosha helps prevent imbalances that could interfere with practice, such as restlessness, heaviness, or mental fog.

4. **Digestibility:**
   - Easily digestible foods are key to preventing lethargy and digestive discomfort, which can disrupt meditation. Focus on foods that are simple yet nourishing, aiding the smooth flow of energy.

Practical Dietary Recommendations for Kriya Yogam Practitioners

1. **Grains and Cereals:**
   - **Examples:** Rice, millets (ragi, bajra), whole wheat, oats.
   - **Why:** These grains are grounding and provide steady energy without overstimulation. Millets and oats are also rich in fiber, which helps regulate blood sugar.
   - **Suggestion:** Try light rice porridge or khichdi (a mixture of rice and lentils) for easy digestion.
2. **Legumes and Lentils:**
   - **Examples:** Moong dal, masoor dal, split urad dal.
   - **Why:** These legumes are high in protein and easier to digest than other beans. They nourish muscles without taxing the digestive system.
   - **Suggestion:** Moong dal soup or lightly spiced masoor dal with cumin and turmeric is a good choice.
3. **Fruits:**
   - **Examples:** Bananas, apples, papaya, mango, pomegranates, seasonal berries.
   - **Why:** Fruits provide quick energy, vitamins, and hydration. They are sattvic and help maintain a light, balanced body.
   - **Suggestion:** Enjoy fresh fruits in the morning to cleanse and energize. Limit acidic fruits (like oranges) to maintain mental clarity.

4. **Vegetables:**
   - **Examples:** Spinach, carrots, beets, sweet potatoes, bottle gourd, pumpkin, green beans.
   - **Why:** Leafy greens and root vegetables support cleansing and balance prana. Avoid overly pungent or tamasic vegetables like garlic and onions.
   - **Suggestion:** Opt for steamed or lightly cooked vegetables, which preserve nutrients and are easy to digest.
5. **Herbs and Spices:**
   - **Examples:** Turmeric, ginger, cumin, coriander, cardamom, fennel.
   - **Why:** Spices like turmeric and ginger improve digestion and circulation, while cardamom and fennel enhance mental clarity.
   - **Suggestion:** Add turmeric to dals or vegetables and drink ginger-fennel tea after meals to aid digestion.
6. **Dairy Products:**
   - **Examples:** Milk, ghee, paneer.
   - **Why:** Dairy is sattvic when consumed in moderation, providing healthy fats and proteins that support meditation. Ghee nourishes the nervous system and helps ground energy.
   - **Suggestion:** Warm milk with turmeric or saffron before bed can promote restful sleep.
7. **Nuts and Seeds:**
   - **Examples:** Almonds, walnuts, sesame seeds, pumpkin seeds.
   - **Why:** Nuts and seeds are rich in healthy fats and proteins, sustaining energy over long periods, making them ideal for meditation practitioners.
   - **Suggestion:** Soaked almonds or walnuts are particularly sattvic and beneficial for brain health.

8. **Hydration:**

   - **Examples:** Warm water, herbal teas (tulsi, chamomile, ginger), coconut water.
   - **Why:** Staying hydrated is crucial for energy flow. Warm water aids digestion, while herbal teas provide calming and rejuvenating effects.
   - **Suggestion:** Start your day with a glass of warm water with lemon for cleansing, and avoid caffeine, which can disrupt meditation.

Foods to Avoid

- **Highly Processed and Fried Foods:** These create lethargy and cloud mental clarity.
- **Heavy or Tamasic Foods:** Foods like garlic, onion, excessively spicy items, and overly sweet foods can disturb inner calm.
- **Caffeine and Sugary Drinks:** These stimulate the mind and can disrupt focus during meditation.

Sample Sattvic Diet Plan for Kriya Yogam Practitioners

- **Morning:** Start with warm water and lemon, followed by fruits or a smoothie made with bananas, soaked almonds, and cardamom.
- **Lunch:** Rice or millets with moong dal, steamed vegetables, and yogurt for probiotic support.
- **Evening:** Herbal tea (tulsi or chamomile) with a handful of nuts or coconut water.
- **Dinner:** Khichdi with vegetables or a light vegetable soup with paneer or cottage cheese.
- **Before Bed:** Warm milk with turmeric for a peaceful mind and restful sleep.

Mindful Eating: "Drink Your Food and Chew Your Water"

Mindful eating is a crucial practice for Kriya Yogam practitioners. "Drink your food and chew your water" means eating with full awareness, thoroughly chewing food to initiate digestion, and sipping water slowly to absorb it gradually. This approach ensures that the body does not have to work too hard to digest, which helps maintain a light and balanced digestive system, essential for deep meditation and energy work.

The Power of Receptivity – Nourishing More Than the Body

The energy your body needs doesn't come solely from food—60% of the energy you require comes from water, air, and sunlight. Your body absorbs energy from these sources, and how you receive this energy can significantly affect your vitality.

When you're joyful, enthusiastic, and open, your body's capacity to use energy increases. On days when you're feeling good, you might notice that you need less food, as your energy is fueled by the positive energy around you. Receptivity to the world around you—embracing life with an open heart—allows energy to flow freely and nourish you beyond what you eat.

To experience this energy shift, let go of control and open yourself to the world. This receptivity helps balance your body and mind, amplifying your spiritual practice and overall well-being.

By adopting a mindful, sattvic diet and cultivating receptivity, Kriya Yogam practitioners can enhance their energy, mental clarity, and spiritual alignment, ultimately supporting their progress on the path to self-realization.

Kriya Amrutham 18

Change doesn't
happen overnight,
so don't expect miracles
to occur in a single day.
You need to take action,
embrace your karma,
and actively work on
shaping your destiny.
Only you can clear
your karma,
it's something you must
do for yourself.

TRANSFORMING YOURSELF

The need for transformation in today's world is undeniable. The fast-paced, interconnected, and often chaotic nature of modern life calls for individuals to undergo significant shifts—not only in how they live but also in how they perceive themselves, others, and the world around them. This transformation can be summarized in the following core areas:

1. **Inner Transformation**

    - **Self-Awareness**: The ability to observe ourselves and our behaviors without judgment allows us to break free from habitual patterns. This leads to greater clarity and conscious decision-making. Kriya Yogam, through meditation and breath control, enhances self-awareness by bringing practitioners into a state of presence and stillness.
    - **Emotional Intelligence**: Emotional regulation, empathy, and understanding our emotions and those of others are key to forming healthy relationships in today's world. The practice of compassion is critical in overcoming division and fostering harmony.
    - **Spiritual Growth**: In a world where external distractions are abundant, reconnecting with the inner self through spiritual practices such as meditation and Yogam provides deeper meaning and balance. Practices like Kriya Yogam facilitate the integration of mind, body, and spirit, allowing practitioners to tap into their higher consciousness.

2. **Mental and Emotional Resilience**

    - **Adaptability and Growth Mindset**: With the constant evolution of technology, climate challenges, and global shifts, maintaining a flexible mindset is essential. Embracing change rather than resisting it allows individuals to thrive in turbulent times.
    - **Self-Compassion and Mental Health Care**: Today, there is a growing recognition of the importance of mental health. Addressing

self-compassion and de-stigmatizing mental health struggles are necessary steps to foster overall well-being.

3. **Ethical and Responsible Living**

    - **Environmental Responsibility**: As we face a climate crisis, the importance of sustainable living practices has never been clearer. By shifting towards mindful consumption and reducing our environmental footprint, we can contribute to a healthier planet.
    - **Mindful Consumption**: Whether it's the food we eat, the media we consume, or the goods we purchase, being mindful of how these choices impact our well-being and the world around us is essential for reducing stress and increasing fulfillment.

4. **Community and Collective Awareness**

    - **Unity and Compassion**: The recognition that we are all interconnected is vital. Compassionate actions—whether in personal relationships or broader societal movements—help bridge gaps and create a more harmonious world.
    - **Service-Oriented Actions**: Serving others, whether through volunteer work or small acts of kindness, strengthens communities and fosters a sense of shared responsibility and connection.

5. **Technological Balance**

    - **Responsible Use of Technology**: While technology has brought significant advancements, it's important to strike a balance between digital engagement and human connection. Mindful use of technology ensures that it enhances, rather than detracts from, our well-being.
    - **Embracing Positive Innovations**: Technological advancements that prioritize humanity's well-being—like innovations in healthcare or education—should be embraced. These have the potential to uplift society as a whole.

6. **Spiritual Connection and Guidance**

    - **Higher Purpose**: In a world where many chase after transient material goals, seeking a higher purpose—such as service to humanity or spiritual fulfillment—can lead to deeper, more lasting fulfillment.
    - **Living by Universal Principles**: Timeless spiritual values such as truth, non-violence, humility, and love provide guidance for ethical living. Aligning our actions with these principles fosters inner peace and contributes to societal well-being.

The One Thing Required for Transformation: Awareness

Awareness stands out as the most crucial ingredient for driving transformation. It's the starting point for change and the lens through which we can see ourselves and the world clearly. Here's how awareness acts as the catalyst for transformation:

- **Self-Understanding**: Awareness enables us to recognize our patterns, limitations, and potential. It allows us to discern what needs transformation—whether in our thoughts, habits, or relationships.
- **Present-Moment Focus**: By being mindful of the present moment, we become less reactive and more intentional in our actions. This mindfulness enables us to align our actions with our deeper values and life's purpose.
- **Inner Motivation**: Awareness fosters intrinsic motivation for change. It encourages us to transform not out of societal pressures, but because we recognize the deeper need for growth and harmony within ourselves.
- **Compassionate Action**: A deeper awareness of the interconnectedness of all life leads to greater empathy and compassion, not just for ourselves but for others. This awareness becomes the foundation for service, kindness, and collective well-being.

- **Connection to the Divine or Higher Self**: Through awareness, we can connect with our true nature and higher consciousness. Spiritual practices, like meditation or Kriya Yogam, heighten this awareness, leading to self-realization and the peace that comes with it.

In essence, awareness is the bedrock of personal and collective transformation. It's through awareness that we understand what needs to change, recognize opportunities for growth, and begin to act with greater compassion and intention. Whether through spiritual practices or daily mindfulness, cultivating awareness is the key to unlocking true transformation in today's rapidly changing world.

Kriya Amrutham 19

Ego

Pay attention to yourself and notice this: Whenever you feel superior or inferior to someone, that's your ego at work.

The ego is the core of our struggles: The weak are controlled by it, the wise have mastered it, and the intelligent are constantly at odds with it.

Ego tells you, "Once everything falls into place, I'll feel at peace." But the spirit whispers, "Find your peace first, and then everything will fall into place."

Misery feeds the ego. That's why you often see so many unhappy people—it keeps them stuck in a cycle. At its core, the ego is just an idea of who you think you are, which you carry with you all the time. If someone corrects you and you feel offended, that's a clear sign your ego is in control. Ego often identifies with things like possessions, your job, social status, recognition, education, physical appearance, talents, relationships, family history, and even beliefs tied to nationality, race, or religion. But none of these things are truly you.

You are not just one person. You are three: The person you think you are, the person others think you are, and the person you truly are.

Chapter 18

Ellaam Maayaai

Ellaam Maayaai (Everything is Illusion) is indeed a central and transformative concept in both spiritual practices and philosophical teachings, especially in Kriya Yogam. Rooted in Advaita Vedanta, which teaches the non-dual nature of existence, the realization of Ellaam Maayaai guides practitioners toward understanding the impermanence of the material world and the eternal nature of the Self.

1. The Meaning of Ellaam Maayaai in Kriya Yogam

Ellaam Maayaai is a Tamil phrase meaning "Everything is Illusion." Maya, in this context, refers to the illusion or deceptive appearance of the material world. It presents reality as separate, permanent, and distinct, when, in fact, everything is interconnected, transient, and a manifestation of the Divine essence. The physical world, therefore, is an illusion because it is constantly changing and subject to destruction, while the ultimate reality, the Atman (Self), or Brahman (the Absolute), remains eternal and unchanging. For Kriya Yogis, understanding this helps to detach from the material world and focus on the realization of the eternal truth.

2. The Role of Maya in the Spiritual Journey

Maya is the force that binds the soul to the cycle of birth and death, creating the illusion of duality and separation. It manifests in various forms:

- **Perception of Duality**: Maya creates the illusion of opposites—pleasure and pain, good and bad, light and dark—keeping us from realizing the inherent unity of all things.

- **Attachment and Desire**: Our attachments to the material world—money, relationships, possessions—are born out of Maya. These attachments are fleeting, and their impermanence leads to suffering.
- **Egoic Identification**: Maya fuels the ego, which identifies with the body, mind, and emotions, and fosters a false sense of individuality. This ego is one of the primary obstacles to spiritual awakening.

The Kriya Yogi aims to transcend these illusions, recognizing the truth that all of creation is part of the Divine. By overcoming Maya, the practitioner can realize that their true nature is not separate from Brahman.

3. Practices to Overcome Maya and Realize Ellaam Maayaai

Kriya Yogam provides specific practices that help practitioners move beyond the illusion of Maya:

- **Meditation (Dhyana)**: Meditation helps to quiet the mind and turn the attention inward. By focusing on the breath or a mantra, Kriya Yogis detach from the distractions of the external world and deepen their awareness of the unchanging inner reality.
- **Pranayama (Breath Control)**: Controlled breathing practices help elevate the prana (life force) and purify the energy channels, dissolving the ego and attachments to the physical body, thus moving the practitioner closer to higher states of consciousness.
- **Self-Inquiry (Atma Vichara)**: By questioning "Who am I?" the practitioner can pierce through the illusion of the self, recognizing that their true essence is beyond the transient body and mind.

- **Kriya Pranayama (Sacred Breathing Techniques)**: Specific techniques such as Kapalbhati, Anulom Vilom, and Kundalini Pranayama are designed to purify the body, mind, and spirit. These practices guide the yogi towards the realization that everything is interconnected and divine.
- **Detachment (Vairagya)**: Detachment from worldly desires is crucial in overcoming Maya. Kriya Yogis practice Vairagya by recognizing the impermanence of material wealth, relationships, and pleasures, cultivating dispassion to create space for spiritual growth.

4. The Illusion of the Material World in Everyday Life

While Kriya Yogis acknowledge the illusory nature of the material world, they do not reject it. The world is seen as a reflection of the divine, and everything in it is a manifestation of Brahman. The illusion lies in how we perceive and interact with the world:

- **Worldly Actions with Spiritual Awareness**: Kriya Yogis continue to engage with the world, but they do so with the awareness that these external realities are temporary. Their true nature is beyond these transient phenomena.
- **Seeing Divinity in All**: Rather than viewing the world as separate and disconnected, Kriya Yogis aim to see the divine presence in all beings and things. This shift in perception helps dissolve the illusion of separation, revealing the underlying unity of all existence.

5. The Ultimate Realization: Oneness with the Divine

The realization of Ellaam Maayaai leads to the profound understanding that there is no separation between the individual soul (Atman) and the Supreme Consciousness (Brahman). The illusion of duality dissolves, and the practitioner experiences unity with the Divine. This is the ultimate goal of Kriya Yogam—Moksha, or liberation, which is the freedom from the cycle of birth and death and the realization of oneness with the Divine.

- **The Role of the Guru**: The Guru plays a vital role in guiding the disciple through the layers of illusion, providing wisdom and practices that accelerate the realization of the ultimate truth.
- **Moksha (Liberation)**: The ultimate goal is liberation from suffering and ignorance. By transcending the illusion of Maya, the Kriya Yogi attains eternal peace, bliss, and unity with the Divine.

6. Conclusion: Ellaam Maayaai in the Path of Kriya Yogam

Ellaam Maayaai is a profound concept for Kriya Yogis, helping them see beyond the material world and recognize the eternal truth that all is one with the Divine. This understanding enables the practitioner to detach from worldly distractions and focus on the inner journey of self-realization. Through practices like meditation, pranayama, and detachment, Kriya Yogis gradually peel away the layers of illusion and awaken to the realization that the world, in its essence, is an illusion pointing toward the eternal truth of unity.

By understanding and applying the concept of Ellaam Maayaai, Kriya Yogis cultivate spiritual insight that transcends the transient material world, ultimately achieving oneness with the Divine and liberation from the cycle of rebirth.

Other side of Ellaam Maayaai

GOD CONSCIOUSNESS

Connecting with God is indeed a deeply personal and transformative journey, and the practices outlined reflect various ways in which we can invite the Divine into our lives. These practices not only lead us closer to God but also cultivate a deeper sense of presence, humility, and connection in our daily experiences.

Meditation and Prayer: The Gateway to the Divine

Meditation, particularly within the framework of Kriya Yogam, is a powerful tool to quiet the mind and access divine consciousness. The stillness found in meditation is where we can experience God's presence. It's in that silence, away from distractions and mental clutter, that we can feel deeply connected to the Divine essence. Prayer, whether formal or informal, structured or spontaneous, also serves as an intimate conversation with God. Through consistent prayer, we open ourselves to divine guidance, allowing patience and perseverance to dissolve obstacles and create space for miracles to unfold.

Mindfulness: Sensing the Divine in Everyday Life

Mindfulness transforms the way we perceive the world, reminding us that every action can be sacred. Living with awareness—seeing the Divine in each moment—invites us to engage with the world from a place of reverence and purpose. Whether it's eating, walking, or speaking, each act can become a prayer when performed with a heart open to the presence of God.

Seva: Connecting with God through Selfless Service

Acts of kindness and compassion, or Seva, provide an avenue for divine connection by dissolving the ego and expanding the heart. When we give without expecting anything in return, we align ourselves with the energy of love and selflessness, which brings us closer to the Divine. Through Seva, we realize that by helping others, we are in fact serving the Divine presence that resides in them.

Sacred Texts: Wisdom to Guide Our Relationship with God

Reading and reflecting on sacred texts like the Bhagavad Gita or the Yogam Sutras provides invaluable insights into the nature of God and the path toward spiritual awakening. These teachings guide us in how to nurture our relationship with the Divine, helping to clarify the mysteries of life and guiding us toward deeper realization.

Kriya Pranayama: Breathing into Divine Awareness

In Kriya Yogam, breathing exercises (Kriya Pranayama) are essential for harmonizing the mind, body, and spirit. Through conscious breathing, we align ourselves with divine energy, transforming our consciousness and facilitating a deeper connection with God. The rhythmic flow of breath serves as a bridge to heightened awareness and spiritual transformation, making the presence of the Divine more tangible within us.

Nature: The Divine Manifested in Creation

Nature often serves as a powerful reminder of God's omnipresence. Whether it's the stillness of a forest, the vastness of the ocean, or the beauty of a sunset, nature reflects the divine order and creativity. By spending time in nature, we can experience a profound sense of connection to the Divine, feeling that we are part of the greater whole. Observing nature with gratitude helps awaken a sense of reverence for the divine presence that surrounds us at all times.

Surrender and Trust: Letting Go and Allowing God to Lead

Surrender is a central practice in many spiritual paths, including Kriya Yogam and devotion to Shiva. It's the act of letting go of control, trusting that a higher power is guiding us. This surrender is not about passivity; it's about faith—faith that God's plan is unfolding and that we are part of it. When we stop resisting life and instead embrace each moment with humility and gratitude, we create space for divine grace to flow freely into our lives.

Shiva Devotion: Living with Divine Awareness

For those devoted to Shiva, the practice of remembering him throughout the day—whether through chanting his name or embodying his qualities—brings a sense of constant connection with the Divine. By reflecting Shiva's values—humility, compassion, kindness—devotees feel the transformative power of these qualities in their lives, gradually shifting their inner reality and becoming conduits of divine grace.

The Illusory Mind and Surrendering to Divine Flow

As you mentioned, the mind is often seen as an illusion in many spiritual traditions. It creates the illusion of separation between us and the Divine. By quieting the mind, through meditation, prayer, and surrender, we allow the barriers of the ego to fall away. This dissolution of mental and egoic boundaries opens us to the truth of divine presence, allowing us to experience miracles that seem to transcend the limits of ordinary life.

Everyday Practices to Invite the Divine

The simple act of offering a chair for God at the dining table or consuming prasad with reverence can be transformative. These actions may seem ordinary, but when done with love, awareness, and the intention to invite the Divine into every moment, they become profound expressions of devotion.

Ultimately, the journey to connect with God is about recognizing His presence in every moment and aligning our actions, thoughts, and feelings with the divine will. Through practices like prayer, meditation, Seva, mindfulness, and surrender, we draw closer to the Divine each day, gradually experiencing the peace, love, and oneness that resides at the heart of all creation.

Kriya Amrutham 20

Self-realization is not just

about listening to teachings,

but truly understanding

God's essence.

True growth comes from

recognizing God's presence

within you.

LIGHT INSIDE YOU

In each of us exists a profound and eternal light—a spark that connects us with the infinite, the source of all consciousness. This light is not just a metaphor but a real, divine energy that permeates every cell, guiding our lives even when we are unaware of it. In this chapter, we'll explore how Kriya Yogam awakens and amplifies this inner light, helping us bridge the gap between our human experience and divine essence.

The Nature of Inner Light

Our inner light is the atman, or soul—a fragment of the Universal Consciousness that resides within. This light reflects pure awareness, bliss, and love, untouched by the fluctuations of the mind or the limitations of our physical bodies. When we live in tune with this light, we experience joy, clarity, and a deep connection with everything around us. However, daily distractions, desires, and doubts often cloud our awareness, obscuring this light. Kriya Yogam offers tools to remove these obstructions, allowing the inner light to shine forth.

Awakening the Inner Light Through Breath

In Kriya Yogam, breath is the key to accessing the light within. Each breath can be seen as a wave that carries prana, the life force energy. Through specific pranayama techniques, we learn to calm the mind and direct this energy inward, allowing us to experience the subtle presence of our inner light.

One advanced practice is the technique of Sushumna Kriya, which channels energy along the central energy pathway in the spine, the Sushumna Nadi. When the prana moves through this channel, it awakens the chakras, igniting the inner light with greater intensity. This energy pathway connects the Muladhara (root) chakra to the Sahasrara (crown) chakra, representing the journey from individual consciousness to universal consciousness. Practitioners often report seeing visions of light, feeling profound bliss, or experiencing an overwhelming sense of unity with the Divine.

The Vision of the Light: A Gateway to Divine Realization

In advanced stages of Kriya practice, some practitioners experience the "Divine Light." This vision appears as a radiant glow within the spiritual eye or third-eye center. Spiritual masters have described this experience as a pivotal moment on the spiritual path, a glimpse of the Divine. It is said that this light is not only seen but felt, permeating the mind and body with an indescribable sense of peace.

One advanced mantra that supports this vision is "Om Jyotir Atman"—a Sanskrit chant that means "I am the light of the soul." By repeating this mantra while visualizing the light at the spiritual eye, the practitioner attunes themselves more deeply to the divine frequency. This mantra amplifies the inner radiance and invokes the energy of Mahavatar Babaji, guiding the practitioner toward a state of deep, silent illumination.

Practices for Amplifying the Light

1. **Kriya Pranayama with Light Visualization**: Inhale deeply, imagining that you're drawing pure white light from the crown down to the Muladhara chakra. As you exhale, feel the light radiate outward, illuminating your whole being. Repeat this with each breath, allowing the light to grow with each cycle.
2. **Meditation on the Third Eye**: Visualize a radiant point of light between the eyebrows, holding your attention there with gentle focus. Allow thoughts to dissolve as you merge your awareness with the light. With time, this practice dissolves the ego's boundaries, revealing a vast, luminous consciousness within.
3. **Silent Reflection on Mahavatar Babaji's Presence**: In a meditative state, visualize Mahavatar Babaji's form as a beacon of light within your heart. This visualization strengthens the connection with his grace, allowing his energy to guide you in your practice. According to Sri M, this act of silent communion with Babaji invites his guidance and blessings into one's journey.

Living with Light: The Transformative Impact of Kriya

As we cultivate this light within, it transforms every aspect of our lives. Relationships are no longer bound by need or expectation; rather, they become expressions of love and compassion. Challenges become opportunities for growth, seen through the lens of divine perspective. This light brings clarity, wisdom, and a profound sense of purpose, lifting us from the mundane to the divine in each moment.

Living in the light of our inner self means embracing a state of constant expansion, where the ordinary becomes sacred and every breath is a step closer to realizing our unity with the cosmos.

This is the promise of Kriya Yogam: to illuminate our inner world so brightly that we cannot help but share that light with others, spreading joy, peace, and love in everything we do.

The light is often described in Kriya Yogam and other yogic practices as residing in a central channel, along a straight path between the Ajna (third eye) and the Sahasrara (crown) chakras. This pathway, which runs from the base of the spine to the crown of the head, is called the Sushumna Nadi.

The light that yogis visualize or perceive often appears to be located at or around the meeting point of the Ajna and the Sahasrara chakras along this vertical line. Some yogis and practitioners experience a "crossing" of energies or an intense merging of light where these two chakras align, which might feel like an intersection or merging of two lines of consciousness—upward from the Ajna and downward from the Sahasrara. This merging is sometimes called the "Bindu" or the "Divine Point," representing a gateway or a bridge between human consciousness (associated with the Ajna chakra) and divine consciousness (associated with the Sahasrara chakra).

In more advanced stages of Kriya, practitioners may experience this intersection as a radiant point where duality dissolves, revealing a unified consciousness or state of divine oneness. The sensation of this light is often described as an indescribable peace or bliss, where one feels connected to a greater cosmic reality.

Final Reflections

The journey to discovering the "Light Inside You" is one of patience, perseverance, and surrender. Each step reveals a deeper truth about who you are and why you're here, leading you to the ultimate realization that the light within is not separate from the divine light outside. Through Kriya Yogam, you're given the gift to reconnect with this eternal essence, to recognize that the light you seek is—and always has been—inside you.

Kriya Amrutham 21

Jeevakarunyam: Compassion for All Life

Jeevakarunyam, the practice of compassion toward all living beings, is a cornerstone of spiritual growth in Kriya Yogam.

It emphasizes the interconnectedness of all life and calls for kindness, non-violence (ahimsa), and respect for nature and animals as expressions of divine energy.

Advanced teachings reveal that practicing Jeevakarunyam purifies the heart and mind, dissolving karmic impressions (samskaras) and fostering inner harmony. Acts of selfless compassion elevate one's vibrational frequency, making the practitioner more receptive to higher spiritual energies during meditation.

This chapter explores how embodying Jeevakarunyam transforms not only the individual but also the environment, reinforcing the spiritual truth that by uplifting others, we uplift ourselves.

Chapter 19

Jeevakarunyam

Jeevakarunyam: Compassion for All Living Beings in Kriya Yogam

Jeevakarunyam, or compassion for all living beings, is a central principle in Kriya Yogam, reflecting a deep empathy and reverence for all forms of life. This practice aligns with key yogic ideals like **ahimsa** (non-violence) and **seva** (selfless service), purifying the heart and mind of the practitioner while also helping them attain unity with universal consciousness.

1. The Concept of Jeevakarunyam in Kriya Yogam

Jeevakarunyam transcends mere ethical behavior—it's a spiritual practice that helps Kriya Yogis recognize the divine essence present in all beings. This recognition fosters a profound connection between the individual (Atman) and the universe (Brahman), reinforcing the yogic philosophy of non-duality. Compassion towards others serves as a tool to deepen the practitioner's spiritual journey, gradually aligning their vibration with higher energies and enhancing their connection to divine consciousness.

- **Unity with the Divine**: Compassion fosters a mindset that transcends personal identity, helping Kriya Yogis unite with the divine.
- **Vibrational Alignment**: Acts of compassion resonate with higher vibrations, aiding spiritual purification and consciousness elevation, which is the goal of Kriya practices.

2. Jeevakarunyam as an Extension of Ahimsa

While **ahimsa** (non-violence) asks us to avoid harm, **Jeevakarunyam** goes further by encouraging active compassion. It's not just about refraining from causing harm; it's about actively nurturing and relieving the suffering of all beings. This active compassion promotes inner peace and prepares the heart for deeper meditation.

- **Beyond Non-Harming to Active Helping**: Practicing Jeevakarunyam involves proactive kindness and service to others.
- **Cultivating Peace**: This practice cultivates a peaceful heart and mind, which is essential for the stillness needed in meditation.

3. Practical Ways to Cultivate Jeevakarunyam

For Kriya Yogis, cultivating Jeevakarunyam involves integrating compassion into everyday actions. Here are some ways to express it:

- **Vegetarianism**: Adopting a vegetarian diet reflects compassion for animals and aligns with a sattvic lifestyle, supporting spiritual practices.
- **Animal Care**: Treating animals with respect, feeding stray animals, or supporting animal sanctuaries nurtures the vibration of compassion.
- **Service to People**: Acts of kindness such as feeding the hungry, helping the elderly, and providing for those in need express Jeevakarunyam in human interactions.
- **Environmental Stewardship**: Protecting the Earth and its ecosystems is a way of showing compassion to all forms of life and aligning with universal harmony.

4. Spiritual Benefits of Practicing Jeevakarunyam

Jeevakarunyam offers numerous spiritual benefits for Kriya Yogis, enhancing their ability to meditate and connect with the Divine.

- **Heart Chakra Activation**: Practicing compassion opens and balances the Anahata (heart) chakra, promoting unconditional love and connection with all beings.
- **Purification of Karma**: Compassionate acts generate positive karma, purifying the practitioner's past actions and reducing attachments that bind them to the cycle of samsara.

- **Dissolution of Ego**: By fostering humility and empathy, Jeevakarunyam helps dissolve the ego, allowing the practitioner to merge with universal consciousness.
- **Enhanced Meditation**: Compassionate actions contribute to a peaceful mind, creating the mental clarity necessary for deep meditation and inner stillness.

5. Jeevakarunyam as a Path to Bhakti

Jeevakarunyam is also a form of **Bhakti** (devotion). For Kriya Yogis, serving others with a compassionate heart is akin to worshiping the Divine within all beings.

- **Service as Worship**: Compassionate service is a form of devotion, where the Yogi sees the Divine in every being and serves them as an expression of love for God.
- **Love as a Transformative Force**: Acts of love and compassion elevate both the giver and the receiver, facilitating spiritual growth and divine connection.

6. Practical Challenges and Insights for Kriya Yogis Practicing Jeevakarunyam

While Jeevakarunyam is deeply beneficial, it presents challenges, especially for those who must maintain a balance between compassion and personal energy preservation. Here are some insights:

- **Setting Boundaries**: Kriya Yogis must balance compassion with self-care, ensuring that their own well-being is not sacrificed in the process of helping others.
- **Detachment in Compassion**: Compassion should be practiced without attachment to outcomes or recognition. This detachment helps transcend ego and encourages selfless service.

- **Mindfulness in Compassion**: Kriya Yogis should practice mindfulness, ensuring their actions are genuinely beneficial and not motivated by personal desires or expectations.

7. Conclusion: Jeevakarunyam as a Foundation for Higher States of Consciousness

Jeevakarunyam is not just a moral principle; it is a vital practice that helps Kriya Yogis purify their energy, transcend their ego, and align with the divine. It supports the spiritual journey by creating harmony between thoughts, actions, and energy. By practicing compassion, the Yogi purifies their karma, transcends individual limitations, and opens themselves to divine grace, moving closer to union with the Divine. Compassion, in this way, becomes a bridge between the individual soul and universal consciousness, fostering profound inner peace, joy, and spiritual liberation.

"Transcending Preferences: Embracing the Divine in All Creation"

This teaching encourages a deep shift in perspective, where the seeker moves beyond personal preferences and embraces the divine presence in all aspects of life, regardless of the form it takes.

1. Transcending Preferences

By transcending likes and dislikes, a major source of attachment and aversion, the seeker avoids creating karma and achieves freedom from the cycle of action and reaction. This shift allows the practitioner to move toward a state of purity and inner peace.

2. Observing Creation with Reverence

In noticing the smallest details of nature, the seeker begins to perceive the divine care woven into all creation. This sense of reverence fosters a profound respect for life, diminishing the ego's sense of separation from the divine.

3. Grace and Availability

Grace is always available, but it can only be received by those who are open and receptive. Embracing all creation as potentially divine, the seeker becomes a vessel for grace, recognizing that God may manifest in any form.

4. Humility and Universal Respect

Respecting all forms of life cultivates humility, which is essential for spiritual growth. Acknowledging that God may appear in any form encourages the seeker to honor all beings, making them open to divine guidance.

In conclusion, this teaching invites the seeker to live a life of universal respect, reverence, and openness, thereby allowing grace to flow freely and guiding them toward spiritual liberation.

Kriya Amrutham 22

Agathiyar teachings on food charity emphasize the deep connection between selfless giving, nourishment, and spiritual growth. He highlighted several key principles:

1. **Selfless Giving:** Agathiyar viewed giving food as a profound act of compassion. It purifies both the giver and the receiver when done with a pure heart, without seeking recognition or reward.
2. **Food as a Divine Gift:** Food is seen as a divine blessing. Sharing it with others honours the divine presence in all beings, acknowledging our interconnectedness.
3. **Purity of Food:** Agathiyar stressed that the food offered should be pure and of good quality. Offering stale or impure food was disrespectful. Charity should reflect care and reverence.
4. **Avoiding Egotism:** Giving food should come from a place of love, not ego. Agathiyar warned against giving with the desire for recognition or superiority. The focus should be on the well-being of the recipient.
5. **Spiritual Benefits:** Feeding others cultivates virtues like empathy, humility, and gratitude. It purifies the giver's heart, aids in spiritual growth, and brings them closer to the divine.
6. **Regular Practice of Giving:** Agathiyar encouraged the consistent practice of charity, especially through food. This builds selflessness and compassion, benefiting both the giver and receiver.
7. **Feeding Spiritual Seekers:** Offering food to spiritual seekers is especially powerful. It yields both material and spiritual benefits, as their high vibrational energy amplifies the goodness of the act.

In essence, Agathiyar taught that food charity is not just about alleviating hunger, but also about nourishing the spirit and deepening the connection with the divine.

Chapter 20

Anna Dhanam

Anna Dhanam (The Practice of Offering Food) and its Role in Kriya Yogam

Anna Dhanam, the practice of offering food, is a revered tradition in Indian spirituality, particularly within the Kriya Yogam tradition. It holds deep spiritual significance, not just as an act of charity but as a form of **seva** (selfless service) and **karma Yogam** (the Yogam of action). This sacred practice extends far beyond simply providing nourishment; it becomes a tool for deepening compassion, purifying karmas, and aiding spiritual growth. Below is a comprehensive exploration of Anna Dhanam's role and its spiritual and practical benefits for Kriya Yogis.

1. Spiritual Significance of Anna Dhanam for Kriya Yogis

For Kriya Yogis, Anna Dhanam represents an offering of love, compassion, and interconnectedness. The practice symbolizes the nourishing of both the physical and spiritual body, recognizing that the divine essence resides in every being. Through this act, Kriya Yogis honor this unity and serve the divine in all forms.

- **Selfless Service (Seva):** Anna Dhanam becomes a form of **seva**, central to Kriya Yogam. Offering food without attachment or expectation cultivates humility, devotion, and detachment, purifying karmas.
- **Sacred Offering (Prasada):** The food offered is often seen as **prasada**—blessed food—imbued with divine energy. This transforms the act of feeding into a sacred ritual that uplifts both giver and receiver.
- **Karma Yoga:** Aligned with **karma yoga**, Anna Dhanam helps the practitioner act without attachment to outcomes. It directs energy into actions that promote the welfare of others, reducing the ego's influence and fostering spiritual evolution.

2. The Yogic Essence of Food in Kriya Practice

In yogic philosophy, food is seen as a carrier of **prana** (life energy). The food offered in Anna Dhanam carries energy that can uplift the recipient's consciousness. Kriya Yogis, who seek to cultivate high prana through practices like **pranayama** (breath control), can channel this energy through the offering of **sattvic** (pure) food.

- **The Three Gunas of Food:**
  - **Sattvic (pure):** Fresh, vegetarian food prepared with a peaceful mind promotes clarity and calmness.
  - **Rajasic (stimulating):** Stimulating food can lead to restlessness and distraction.
  - **Tamasic (heavy):** Stale, processed, or overly fatty food leads to inertia.

For Anna Dhanam, Kriya Yogis typically offer **sattvic** food, supporting spiritual clarity and calmness.

3. Anna Dhanam as an Expression of Ahimsa (Non-Violence)

Ahimsa, or non-violence, is a cornerstone of Kriya Yogam. Anna Dhanam, particularly when offering **vegetarian food**, upholds the principle of **ahimsa**, which avoids causing harm to animals and encourages a peaceful, compassionate lifestyle.

- **Promoting Ahimsa:** Serving vegetarian food encourages compassion toward all beings and reduces violence in the world, contributing to the yogi's spiritual progress.
- **Impact on Collective Consciousness:** The practice subtly promotes vegetarianism, encouraging others to embrace a more harmonious lifestyle, which benefits both the practitioner and the world at large.

4. Ritual Aspects of Anna Dhanam for Kriya Yogis

Anna Dhanam can also take on a ritualistic form, transforming it into a spiritual practice that aligns with the goals of Kriya Yogam. This is achieved through mindfulness and reverence in every step of the offering.

- **Preparation:** Food should be prepared with a pure mind in a clean space. Yogis may chant mantras or offer prayers during preparation to infuse the food with positive energy.
- **Offering as Prasada:** Once prepared, the food can be offered to the divine or a deity, turning the act of feeding into a sacred ritual of surrender and gratitude.
- **Serving with Devotion:** While serving, Kriya Yogis recognize the divine presence within each person they feed, treating them with love and respect as manifestations of the divine.

5. Benefits of Anna Dhanam for Spiritual Progress

Anna Dhanam offers several profound spiritual benefits, which help Kriya Yogis purify their minds, dissolve ego, and progress on their spiritual path.

- **Purification of Karma:** By engaging in Anna Dhanam, practitioners redirect their actions for the benefit of others, purifying past karmas and bringing inner peace.
- **Expansion of Compassion:** The practice fosters deep compassion, opening the **Anahata** (heart) chakra and allowing the yogi to feel unity and love for all beings.
- **Dissolution of Ego:** Serving others selflessly diminishes the ego, allowing for greater humility and a deeper connection to the divine.
- **Inner Contentment and Peace:** Providing nourishment with pure intention brings satisfaction and joy, fostering a sense of fulfillment that arises from helping others.

6. Practical Tips for Practicing Anna Dhanam for Kriya Yogis

To integrate Anna Dhanam into their spiritual practice, Kriya Yogis can follow these practical tips:

- **Offer Pure, Vegetarian Food:** Only offer fresh, vegetarian, and sattvic food to maintain the alignment with **ahimsa**.
- **Infuse Positive Energy:** Keep a peaceful mind while preparing the food. Practicing **pranayama** or chanting mantras can help infuse the food with positive vibrations.
- **Serve with Humility:** Approach each person with reverence, seeing the divine within them and treating them with love.
- **Regular Offerings:** Engage in Anna Dhanam during special occasions, auspicious days, or on a regular basis to deepen the karmic benefits.
- **Express Gratitude:** After serving, express gratitude for the opportunity to help others, reinforcing the attitude of **detachment** and **selflessness**.

7. Conclusion: Anna Dhanam as a Path to Enlightenment

In Kriya Yogam, Anna Dhanam is more than just feeding others—it is a profound spiritual practice. Through this selfless act, Kriya Yogis purify their minds, reduce karmic burdens, and deepen their connection with the divine essence within all beings. This practice not only supports spiritual progress but also fosters compassion, humility, and a greater sense of unity with the universe.

By incorporating Anna Dhanam into their daily lives, Kriya Yogis not only nourish others but also cultivate the qualities needed for the ultimate goal of Kriya Yogam: **self-realization** and **union with the Divine**.

Kriya Amrutham 23

A Gateway to Divine Energy

The Thiruchendur Murugan Temple, dedicated to Lord Murugan, is a sacred site imbued with powerful spiritual vibrations. Situated near the seashore, this temple represents the victory of divine forces over negativity, symbolized by Lord Murugan's conquest of the demon Surapadman.

In Kriya Yogam, Thiruchendur is revered not only for its mythological significance but also for its unique energy fields. Advanced practitioners often speak of the temple's ability to amplify inner stillness and aid in the awakening of Kundalini energy. The alignment of the temple with cosmic energies enhances meditation, making it an ideal space for deep spiritual practice.

This chapter highlights the temple as a bridge between the material and the divine, offering insights into how sacred sites like Thiruchendur Murugan Temple support the spiritual journey through their subtle yet transformative energies.

Chapter 21

Thiruchendur Murugan Temple

A Journey Through Sacred Energies

The Thiruchendur Murugan Temple is more than just a destination or a place of worship—it's an experience, a spiritual journey that invites us to connect with the deeper, powerful energies of the universe. Built with intricate, timeless knowledge, this temple doesn't just exist in the physical realm; it mirrors the internal spiritual path found within each of us. Just as our own bodies hold centers of energy known as chakras, this temple aligns to evoke and elevate these energies, reflecting an ancient wisdom that blends seamlessly with the principles of Kriya Yogam.

When you step into the Thiruchendur Murugan Temple, it feels as if each part of the structure speaks to a different layer of your being, guiding you step by step along a sacred path from the base of earthly grounding to the vastness of divine consciousness. This sacred alignment isn't random; it's intentional, crafted by those who understood the architecture of the body, mind, and spirit, and how these parts can lead to higher consciousness. It's as though every stone, every corner, and every chamber in this temple is there to lead you on a journey through your own inner world.

Just like Kriya Yogam, where energy is transformed and refined step by step through the chakras, the temple provides a space for profound inner transformation. As you walk through the temple, you may sense your own inner energies stirring, responding to the subtle vibrations within the structure. The temple's design itself seems to act as a guide, encouraging this inner awakening and helping devotees connect more deeply with their spiritual essence. It becomes not just a physical walk through the halls of the temple, but a walk inward, into the self.

At the temple, you may feel as though you're being called to move beyond the everyday thoughts and concerns of the world outside and turn toward something deeper. Each step and each gaze upon the temple statues and carvings invites a gentle but powerful shift within. As you stand before the deity, you're reminded that the journey is more than an external pilgrimage; it's a journey within, a journey that speaks to the same truths as Kriya Yogam, where the ultimate goal is unity with the Divine.

For many who visit, the experience of this temple is profoundly transformative. It's a place where both body and soul find peace, where the soul awakens, and where one is drawn closer to the divine. Thiruchendur Murugan Temple becomes not only a place of worship but a living symbol of the inner journey—a sacred space that reflects the deepest longings of the spirit and helps each visitor come closer to their own inner light and ultimate oneness with the universe.

Many temples in India are designed with profound knowledge of spiritual principles, including the chakras and the five elements (Pancha Bhutas), which are foundational to both Yoga and Tantra. In yogic philosophy, temples are often seen as reflections of the human energy body. Their symbolic architecture is intended to guide devotees on a journey of spiritual ascent, similar to Lord Murugan, the deity symbolizing wisdom, spiritual triumph, and the path to enlightenment.

If you're curious about how temples are designed to reflect spiritual ideas, there are plenty of resources to explore. Books on South Indian temple architecture and studies on Hindu iconography, along with the concept of Aarupadai Veedu (the six sacred abodes of Lord Murugan), can offer deeper insights. You can also find interpretations of temple symbolism in works by authors focusing on Indian philosophy and spirituality. Additionally, there are scholarly papers that look at how sacred geometry, temple layout, and chakra symbolism are all connected.

The Thiruchendur Murugan Temple (Thiruchendur Murugar Koil) is an incredibly important pilgrimage site dedicated to Lord Murugan, also known as Kartikeya or Subramanya. It's one of the six Aarupadai Veedu, the sacred abodes of Murugan in Tamil Nadu. Situated on the Bay of Bengal's coastline, this temple's unique architecture and structure are aligned in such a way that they symbolically represent the energy of the seven chakras. It serves as a beautiful architectural and spiritual guide to the inner journey of awakening.

Here's how the seven chakras are thought to be symbolically represented in the design and layout of the Thiruchendur Murugan Temple:

To activate the seven chakras, you need to visit the Thiruchendur Murugan Temple. As you walk through the temple, each chakra is believed to open gradually.

According to the Sidhargal (the enlightened sages), every chakra has the potential to do both good and bad. It's important to understand and accept both aspects. However, when practicing Kriya, the focus should be on cultivating the positive energy of each chakra.

1. Muladhara Chakra (Root Chakra) – Temple Entrance and Surrounding Land

- **Significance:** The Muladhara Chakra is the foundation of the body, representing security, stability, and connection to the Earth. (Good side and bad side of Creating Sexual Power) feeling activation starts.
- **Symbolic Presence:** The entrance of the Thiruchendur Temple, located near the coastline, embodies the qualities of the Root Chakra. The land surrounding the temple, with its connection to the Earth and the ocean, grounds devotees and represents stability and security. Pilgrims arriving at the temple entrance feel rooted in the powerful energy of the Earth, setting the foundation for their spiritual ascent.

2. Svadhisthana Chakra (Sacral Chakra) – Sacred Waters and Bathing Area. (Creates Dhiryam and Adhiryam) Fear and fearlessness

- **Significance**: The Svadhisthana Chakra is associated with water, emotions, creativity, and purification.
- **Symbolic Presence**: The temple has sacred waters nearby, where devotees customarily bathe before entering the temple. This purification ritual represents the Sacral Chakra's cleansing and transformative qualities. The act of washing away impurities symbolizes the release of emotional burdens and desires, preparing devotees to ascend to higher spiritual centers with clarity and purity.

3. Manipura Chakra (Solar Plexus Chakra) – Main Temple Structure and Inner Sanctum. (Creates Good food and Bad food) Lost wealth and give me wealth.

- **Significance**: The Manipura Chakra is the power center, symbolizing willpower, confidence, and the transformative Fire element.
- **Symbolic Presence**: The central structure of the Thiruchendur Temple, housing the sanctum sanctorum, represents the Solar Plexus Chakra. Here, Lord Murugan's main shrine radiates with transformative energy, symbolizing the fire of inner willpower, courage, and personal empowerment. Worship in this area ignites the inner fire within devotees, purifying their ego and empowering them with divine will.

4. Anahata Chakra (Heart Chakra) – The Sanctum and the Idol of Lord Murugan. (Creates Annbu and Veruppu) Family welfare.

- **Significance**: The Heart Chakra represents love, compassion, harmony, and the Air element.

- **Symbolic Presence:** The sanctum of Lord Murugan, situated within the main structure, embodies the qualities of the Heart Chakra. It is here that devotees experience deep devotion and a connection to the divine, promoting qualities of love, compassion, and inner harmony. The presence of Lord Murugan in the sanctum represents the universal love and protection he offers, resonating with the Anahata Chakra's energy of unconditional love.

5. Vishuddha Chakra (Throat Chakra) – Chanting and Prayers Within the Temple. (Creates Poison and Amruth) Destroy the enemy.

- **Significance**: The Vishuddha Chakra governs communication, purity, and self-expression and is connected to the Ether (Space) element.
- **Symbolic Presence**: In the temple, devotees engage in chanting, mantras, and devotional singing, which aligns with the Throat Chakra. The resonance of sacred sounds and chanting within the temple creates an atmosphere of spiritual purity and devotion, uplifting the voices of the devotees and symbolically opening the Throat Chakra. This space allows pilgrims to express their devotion, communicate with the Divine, and purify their hearts and minds.

6. Ajna Chakra (Third Eye Chakra) – Murugan's Divine Vision and the Inner Sanctity.(Creates Good Power and Bad Power) This chakra opens when you see Lord Muruga. Close your eyes and place the image between your two eyes.

- **Significance**: The Ajna Chakra is the center of intuition, wisdom, and insight and is associated with the mind.
- **Symbolic Presence**: Murugan is often associated with divine vision and insight, depicted with his peacock, the sacred spear (Vel), and his wise gaze. In Thiruchendur, the sacred Vel is given a special place, symbolizing the piercing of ignorance and the awakening

of divine wisdom. This corresponds to the Ajna Chakra, inviting devotees to develop their inner vision and intuition as they come before the deity.

7. Sahasrara Chakra (Crown Chakra) – Tower Above the Sanctum (Vimana) and Connection to Divine Consciousness.(Creates Nanri vunarvi and Saabam) When you come out happily outside the temple, this chakra will open.

- **Significance**: The Sahasrara Chakra represents enlightenment, divine consciousness, and the transcendence of individual identity.
- **Symbolic Presence**: The temple's tower or *vimana* above the sanctum represents the Crown Chakra, the gateway to divine consciousness. The vimana is constructed with specific geometries that draw spiritual energy upward and symbolize the soul's ascent toward union with the Divine. When devotees enter this space, they experience the powerful energy of the Sahasrara, invoking divine grace and connecting them with Lord Murugan's consciousness.

Pancha Bhuta Lingams

The Pancha Bhutas, or the Five Great Elements, are directly connected to five sacred temples in South India that are dedicated to Lord Shiva. These temples, known as the Pancha Bhoota Sthalas or Pancha Bhuta Lingams, represent one of the five elements: Earth, Water, Fire, Air, and Ether (Space). These temples symbolize Shiva's manifestation in nature, showing how the divine is present in every element, highlighting the unity between the material world and the spiritual realm.

Here's a look at the five temples and the elements they represent:

1. **Ekambareswarar Temple (Earth) – Kanchipuram, Tamil Nadu**
    - **Element**: Earth (Prithvi)
    - **Description**: The Ekambareswarar Temple represents the Earth element. Located in Kanchipuram, it features a sacred mango tree believed to be over 3,000 years old, symbolizing fertility and grounding—essential qualities of the Earth. The temple's lingam is made of sand, further connecting it to the Earth element.
    - **Spiritual Significance**: Earth represents stability, fertility, and sustenance. Devotees visit to seek grounding, stability, and balance in their lives.
2. **Jambukeswarar Temple (Water) – Thiruvanaikaval, Tamil Nadu**
    - **Element**: Water (Apas)
    - **Description**: This temple is dedicated to the Water element. An underground spring constantly flows around the lingam, symbolizing the fluidity and adaptability of water.
    - **Spiritual Significance**: Water represents emotions, adaptability, and purification. This temple is visited by those seeking emotional cleansing, purification of the mind, and healing in their life circumstances.
3. **Arunachaleswarar Temple (Fire) – Tiruvannamalai, Tamil Nadu**
    - **Element**: Fire (Agni)
    - **Description**: Arunachaleswarar Temple is associated with the Fire element. It sits at the base of the sacred Arunachala Hill, revered as an embodiment of Shiva in the form of fire. During the Karthigai Deepam festival, a massive fire is lit atop the hill, symbolizing Shiva as an eternal flame.

- **Spiritual Significance**: Fire represents transformation, energy, and purification. Devotees come to the temple seeking transformation and purification, burning away ignorance and ego in the fiery energy of Shiva.

4. **Sri Kalahasti Temple (Air) – Srikalahasti, Andhra Pradesh**

    - **Element**: Air (Vayu)
    - **Description**: Dedicated to the Air element, the Sri Kalahasti Temple features a lingam that naturally vibrates with the movement of air, symbolizing Shiva's presence in the form of the invisible, formless air.
    - **Spiritual Significance**: Air represents movement, breath, and freedom. Devotees visit this temple to balance their prana (life force) and achieve mental clarity and liberation from attachment.

5. **Nataraja Temple (Ether/Space) – Chidambaram, Tamil Nadu**

    - **Element**: Ether (Space) (Akasha)
    - **Description**: The Nataraja Temple is dedicated to the Ether or Space element. It is unique because it honors Shiva in the form of Nataraja, the cosmic dancer, symbolizing the dance of creation and destruction in the infinite vastness of space. The sanctum includes an empty space representing Shiva's formless aspect.
    - **Spiritual Significance**: Ether symbolizes the boundless, unbounded consciousness and is the most subtle of the five elements. Devotees visit to experience the essence of divine consciousness and to connect with the infinite, formless aspect of Shiva.

Summary of the Pancha Bhoota Sthalas and Their Significance

The Pancha Bhoota Sthalas are more than just sacred temples; they are metaphysical representations of the five elements in nature and the human body. Each temple embodies Shiva's divine presence within one of the elements—Earth, Water, Fire, Air, and Ether. Visiting these temples is believed to help devotees connect with the corresponding element within themselves, harmonizing their energies, transcending earthly limitations, and recognizing the divine nature of both the physical and spiritual realms. This balance leads to purification and spiritual progress, making the pilgrimage to these temples a deeply transformative experience.

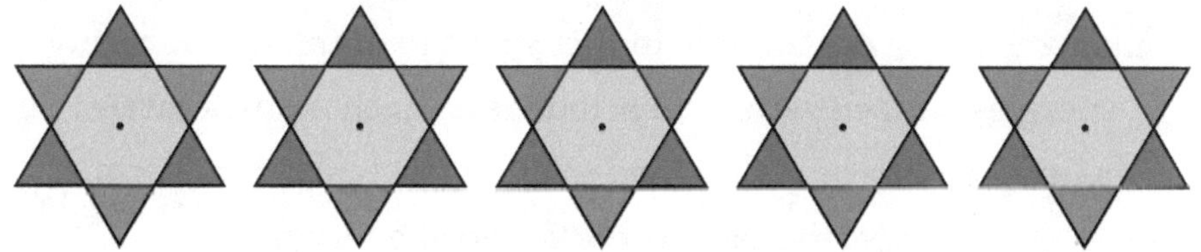

Kriya Amrutham 24

The Power of Divine Sound

Mantras are sacred sound vibrations that act as bridges between the human mind and the divine. In Kriya Yogam, mantras play a central role in focusing the mind, harmonizing energies, and elevating consciousness. Each mantra carries a unique vibration, designed to align the practitioner with specific aspects of universal energy.

Advanced teachings reveal that chanting or meditating on mantras not only calms the mind but also purifies the subtle body by activating nadis (energy channels) and chakras. The repetition of mantras (japa) creates powerful resonance within, awakening dormant spiritual energies like Kundalini Shakti.

This chapter explores how mantras transcend the intellectual mind, connecting practitioners to deeper realms of awareness and guiding them toward self-realization. By understanding the science of sound, one can unlock the transformative potential of these divine syllables.

MANTRAS

Mantras are vibrational tools rooted in the ancient science of sound. They serve as keys to transcend the conscious mind, harmonizing the vibrational energy within and around us. The word "mantra" originates from the Sanskrit roots "manas" (mind) and "tra" (tool or instrument), signifying their role as a tool for mental and spiritual transformation.

Mantras are composed of specific syllables, each carrying unique frequencies that resonate with certain aspects of the cosmos and the inner self. Their power lies in the vibrational quality and the intention behind their repetition. Advanced practitioners recognize that mantras act as energetic pathways to align the practitioner with higher states of consciousness.

The Role of Mantras in Kriya Yogam

In Kriya Yogam, mantras are a vital element of the practice. They are not merely words or sounds but sacred vibrations that align the practitioner with the universal life force (prana) and divine presence. Kriya Yogam integrates mantras as part of a holistic approach that includes breath control, meditation, and self-discipline.

1. **Mantras as Pranic Activators:** Specific mantras in Kriya Yogam are chanted or mentally intoned to activate the subtle energy centers (chakras). This enhances the flow of prana, aiding in the purification of the nadis (subtle energy channels).
2. **Integration with Breath:** Mantras in Kriya Yogam are often synchronized with breath cycles. For instance, mentally chanting So on inhalation and Ham on exhalation aligns the practitioner with the natural rhythm of life and universal consciousness.
3. **Awakening Kundalini Energy:** Advanced Kriya practitioners may use bija mantras (seed sounds) like Om, Hreem, or Kreem

to awaken and guide the dormant Kundalini energy through the spinal column toward the crown chakra (Sahasrara).

4. **Mantra Meditation:** Silent repetition of specific mantras helps focus the mind, dissolve ego-based thoughts, and facilitate deeper states of meditation. This practice enhances the connection with the divine source.

Mantras for Lord Shiva

Lord Shiva is often associated with transformation and inner awakening. His mantras resonate with the universal energy of destruction and renewal, guiding practitioners to dissolve ignorance and realize their eternal essence.

1. **Panchakshari Mantra:**

   Om Namah Shivaya

   This is the most powerful mantra of Lord Shiva. It means "I bow to Shiva," representing surrender to the divine.

2. **Mahamrityunjaya Mantra:**

   Om Tryambakam Yajamahe Sugandhim Pushtivardhanam |

   Urvaarukamiva Bandhanaan Mrityor Mokshiya Maamritaat ||

   This mantra invokes Shiva as the healer, protector, and liberator. This mantra is known as the "Death Conquering Mantra." It is a powerful prayer for healing, protection, and the removal of negative karmic influences. Chanting this mantra helps free the devotee from the bonds of life and death, leading to liberation (moksha) from the cycle of birth and rebirth.

3. **Shiva Gayatri Mantra:**

   Om Tatpurushaya Vidmahe Mahadevaya Dhimahi |

   Tanno Rudra Prachodayat ||

   This mantra helps in attaining spiritual wisdom and removing inner obstacles.

Mantras for Lord Murugan

Lord Murugan, also known as Kartikeya or Skanda, symbolizes divine valor and the power to overcome challenges. His mantras are chanted for protection, wisdom, and spiritual victory.

1. **Om Saravana Bhava**

   This mantra is a powerful invocation to Lord Murugan (also called Kartikeya or Skanda), the divine protector and remover of obstacles. It is believed that chanting "Om Saravana Bhava" with sincere devotion helps devotees clear away past karmas, negative energies, and challenges. The mantra works to bring clarity and purification, aiding in the release of old karmic patterns and guiding the devotee toward liberation. As you chant, you are spiritually aligned with Murugan's grace, helping you move forward on your path with ease and wisdom.

2. **Kandha Shashti Kavacham (Short Form):**

   Om Vel Vetrivel |

   Muruganukku Harohara ||

   This is a powerful chant to seek protection and courage in life's battles.

3. **Murugan Gayatri Mantra:**

   Om Tatpurushaya Vidmahe Mahasenaya Dhimahi |

   Tanno Shanmukha Prachodayat ||

   This mantra enhances wisdom, courage, and victory over negativity.

4. **"Vinai Oda Vidum Katir Vel Maraven"**

   This beautiful line translates to "I shall never forget the Radiant Spear that removes all karmas (or sins)." It is an expression of deep devotion to Lord Murugan's divine weapon, the Vel, which holds immense power. The Vel symbolizes Murugan's ability to dissolve karmas, remove obstacles, and eliminate negativity from the lives of his devotees. By remembering the Katir Vel (the Radiant Spear) and seeking connection with it, devotees ask for Murugan's grace to release them from the chains of suffering and past misdeeds, helping them to live free from the weight of karma.

Advanced Practices:

1. **Silent Repetition (Ajapa Japa):** Advanced practitioners are encouraged to practice Ajapa Japa, the silent, effortless repetition of mantras, aligning them with the natural flow of breath and awareness.
2. **Resonance with Chakras:** Chant mantras like Om Namah Shivaya while focusing on specific chakras, starting from the root (Muladhara) and moving upward to the crown (Sahasrara). This intensifies energy alignment.
3. **Integration with Visualization:** Combine mantra chanting with visualizing the deity or an inner light. For example, while chanting Om Namah Shivaya, imagine a radiant light at the third eye center (Ajna chakra), representing Shiva's omnipresence.
4. **Bija Mantras:** Utilize seed sounds like Hreem (divine power), Kreem (transformation), or Shreem (prosperity and beauty) to deepen meditation and energy alignment.

Mantras are not merely a practice; they are a way of life in spiritual paths like Kriya Yogam. Their vibrations purify the mind, elevate consciousness, and bring practitioners closer to the divine essence within. By dedicating oneself to the disciplined use of mantras, one discovers their immense power to transform life into a continuous state of meditation and joy.

Mantras for Mahavatar Babaji:

While there isn't a universally established mantra exclusively dedicated to Mahavatar Babaji, practitioners often use mantras that align with his energy and teachings. Mahavatar Babaji, regarded as an immortal yogi and a divine guide in the Kriya Yogam tradition, embodies unconditional love, supreme wisdom, and transcendental spiritual power. Below are some mantras that resonate with his essence and are used by his devotees to connect with him:

1. **Om Kriya Babaji Nama Aum**
   Meaning: "I bow to the divine Kriya Babaji."

   This is the most popular mantra used to invoke Mahavatar Babaji's presence and blessings. It aligns the practitioner with his infinite wisdom and transformative energy, promoting spiritual awakening and inner peace.

2. **Om Babaji Namah**

   Meaning: "I bow to Babaji."

   A simple yet powerful mantra that fosters humility and surrender, helping the devotee establish a direct connection with Babaji's grace.

3. **Om Hreem Kriya Babaji Namaha**

   Meaning: "I offer my reverence to Babaji, the divine master of Kriya Yogam."

   The addition of the bija (seed) mantra Hreem amplifies the vibrational potency, invoking divine power and higher consciousness.

4. **Babaji Gayatri Mantra:**

   Om Tatpurushaya Vidmahe

   Kriya Yogeshwaraya Dhimahi

   Tanno Babaji Prachodayat

   Meaning: "Let us meditate on the supreme being who is the master of Kriya Yogam. May Babaji illuminate our intellect and guide us on the spiritual path."

This mantra embodies the divine light of Mahavatar Babaji and is ideal for meditation and spiritual elevation.

Advanced Practices for Babaji's Mantras

1. **Meditative Chanting:** Chant the mantra 108 times daily while focusing on Babaji's image, a radiant light, or the third eye (Ajna Chakra).
2. **Kriya Synchronization:** Integrate the mantra with breathwork, silently intoning it during the inhalation and exhalation cycles to deepen inner stillness and devotion.
3. **Silent Invocation (Ajapa Japa):** Practice the mantra mentally without external sound, aligning it with the natural rhythm of your breath. This helps deepen your awareness of Babaji's omnipresence.
4. **Heart Connection:** Visualize Babaji in your heart center (Anahata Chakra) while chanting. Feel his unconditional love and guidance radiating through your entire being.

By sincerely chanting these mantras, devotees invoke Mahavatar Babaji's transformative energy, fostering spiritual growth and aligning with the divine purpose of life. His grace flows to those who approach him with humility, faith, and devotion.

The Shankam (Conch): A Sacred Symbol and Instrument

The Shankam, or conch shell, holds immense significance in Indian spirituality, mythology, and rituals. It is revered as a sacred object that embodies purity, auspiciousness, and divine energy. Found in the ocean, the Shankam is considered a natural gift from the waters, symbolizing the cosmic sound Om and the divine creation of the universe.

Significance in Spirituality

1. **Symbol of Divine Sound:**

   The Shankam is believed to produce the primordial sound of the universe, Om, when blown. This sound resonates with the cosmic vibration, symbolizing creation and universal harmony.

2. **Representation of Elements:**

   The Shankam represents the element of water (Jala), which is vital for life and sustenance. Its spiral structure signifies the infinite cycles of birth, life, and death.

3. **Instrument of Purification:**

   The blowing of the Shankam during rituals is said to cleanse the environment of negative energies and create a sacred atmosphere, purifying the mind and soul.

Mythological and Religious Importance

1. **Association with Vishnu:**

   In Hindu mythology, Lord Vishnu holds the Shankam named Panchajanya in his upper left hand. It is a divine weapon and an instrument used to announce the beginning of dharmic endeavors. Blowing it is symbolic of invoking divine blessings and proclaiming righteousness.

2. **Role in Epics:**

   In the Mahabharata, the Shankam played a significant role in the Kurukshetra war. Lord Krishna's conch, Panchajanya, and the conches of the Pandavas announced the commencement of the battle and filled their troops with courage and determination.

3. **Symbol of Prosperity:**

   The Shankam is also associated with Goddess Lakshmi, the deity of wealth and abundance. The left-handed conch shells, known as Vamavarti Shankam, are especially revered for attracting prosperity and positive energy.

The Shankam in Rituals and Yoga

1. **Blowing the Shankam**:

   The act of blowing the Shankam is considered an auspicious practice. It strengthens the lungs and respiratory system while also calming the mind. In a spiritual context, the vibration aligns the practitioner with higher frequencies.

2. **Water Purification**:

   Water poured into the Shankam during rituals is considered sacred and used for purification purposes. This water, infused with the conch's energy, is believed to have healing and rejuvenating properties.

3. **Meditative Focus**:

   The Shankam's shape and sound are often used in meditation to represent the spiral journey of spiritual evolution and the resonance of inner stillness.

Varieties of Shankam

1. **Dakshinavarti Shankam**:

   Spirals to the right and is rare. It is associated with Lord Vishnu and symbolizes spiritual protection and divine grace.

2. **Vamavarti Shankam**:

   Spirals to the left and is commonly used in rituals. It represents material prosperity and abundance.

3. **Ganesha Shankam**:

   Resembles the form of Lord Ganesha and is considered a symbol of wisdom and obstacle removal.

Advanced Spiritual Practices with the Shankam

1. **Sound Healing:**

   The vibrations from a blown Shankam can be used in sound therapy to cleanse the chakras and promote energetic balance. The sound activates the throat chakra (*Vishuddha*) and facilitates clear communication with the divine.

2. **Meditation on Omkara:**

   Practitioners meditate on the *Om* vibration produced by the Shankam, merging their consciousness with the universal sound of creation.

3. **Chakra Alignment:**

   When held and focused upon, the spiral structure of the Shankam helps in visualizing the flow of energy through the chakras, aiding in Kundalini awakening.

Conclusion

The Shankam is not just a physical object but a bridge between the material and spiritual realms. It embodies the essence of cosmic vibration, purity, and auspiciousness. Revered across cultures and traditions, the Shankam continues to inspire awe, devotion, and spiritual exploration, making it a timeless symbol of divine connection.

Kriya Amrutham 25

Conclusion

The Eternal Journey Within

As you turn the final page of this book, dear reader, you stand at the threshold of an eternal journey. Kriya Yogam is not merely a practice—it is a profound science of self-realization, a map leading you to the uncharted realms of your inner world. For the beginner, this may feel like the first steps onto a vast and mysterious path. Yet, even the smallest step towards self-awareness carries the potential to transform your life in ways unimaginable.

Advanced Insights on the Path of Kriya

Kriya Yogam begins with the breath, but it is ultimately a gateway to realms beyond the physical. As you deepen your practice, you may experience moments of clarity that transcend the intellect—glimpses of the divine presence within and around you. This is no accident but a natural consequence of aligning yourself with the universal rhythms of life.

One of the advanced principles of Kriya Yogam is the understanding that prana (life force) is the bridge between the body, mind, and spirit. With dedicated practice, the breath evolves from a simple tool for relaxation into a vehicle for profound inner transformation. The techniques you have learned here are designed to harmonize the flow of prana within you, enabling higher states of awareness.

The Sacred Union of Inner Energies

A key milestone in advanced Kriya practice is the awakening of the divine energies within: the union of Shiva (pure consciousness) and Shakti (dynamic energy). This union, symbolized by the ascending energy through

the spinal centers, or chakras, is a pivotal experience that reveals the interconnectedness of all existence. While these terms may seem abstract now, as you continue to practice, you will come to understand them as living truths within your own being.

Trust the Inner Guru

One of the greatest teachings of Mahavatar Babaji and other enlightened masters is the presence of the Inner Guru. While external guidance is invaluable, the ultimate source of wisdom lies within you. Every breath, every moment of silence, and every challenge on the path is an opportunity for the Inner Guru to guide you closer to your divine essence. Cultivate a relationship with this inner presence, trusting that it will lead you to the truth.

Advice for the Journey Ahead

1. **Consistency Over Intensity**: Spiritual growth is not a sprint but a marathon. Even a few minutes of Kriya practice daily can yield profound results over time. Prioritize consistency over intensity.
2. **Integrate, Don't Isolate**: Let your practice inform and enrich your daily life. Whether you are at work, with family, or alone in contemplation, let the peace and awareness cultivated through Kriya permeate your actions.
3. **Be Patient with Yourself**: Progress on the spiritual path is not always linear. There will be moments of doubt, frustration, and stagnation. Embrace these as part of the journey, knowing that each experience is a stepping stone.
4. **Seek Sangha**: Surround yourself with like-minded individuals who uplift and inspire you. Spiritual companionship can provide encouragement, perspective, and a shared sense of purpose.

5. **Stay Open to Grace**: Beyond techniques and discipline lies the mysterious realm of divine grace. Be open to the unexpected blessings and synchronicities that guide you on your path.

The Light Inside You

In the end, all spiritual practices, including Kriya Yogam, point to one eternal truth: the light you seek is already within you. Mahavatar Babaji's timeless message is that you are not separate from the divine but an expression of it. Each breath, each moment, is an opportunity to realize this truth and live it fully.

Take what you have learned here and make it your own. Practice with sincerity, live with awareness, and walk the path with courage and humility. The journey is endless, but every step is worth it.

As the great masters remind us, the goal is not somewhere far away. It is here, now, within you. All you need to do is turn inward and behold the infinite. And so, the journey begins a new.

Om Sri Sai Nathaya Namah
"Om Hreem Sri Gurubyo Namah"
"Lord Muruga of Thiruchendur, please bless us."
Shiva is music, Shiva is dance,
Shiva is song, everything is Him,
Om Namasivaya, Om Namasivaya
Om Namasivaya, Om Namasivaya

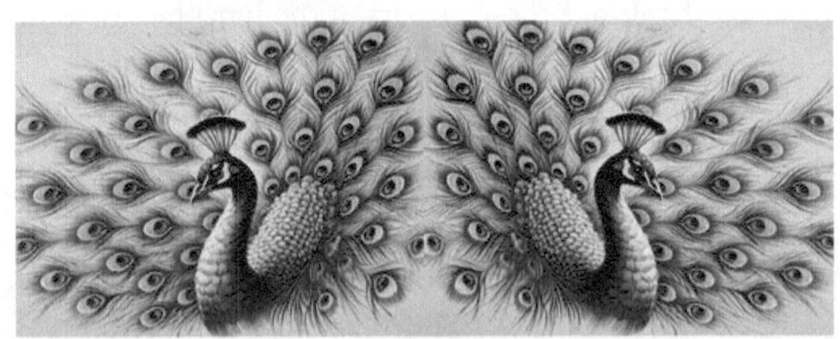

Sri Chakram

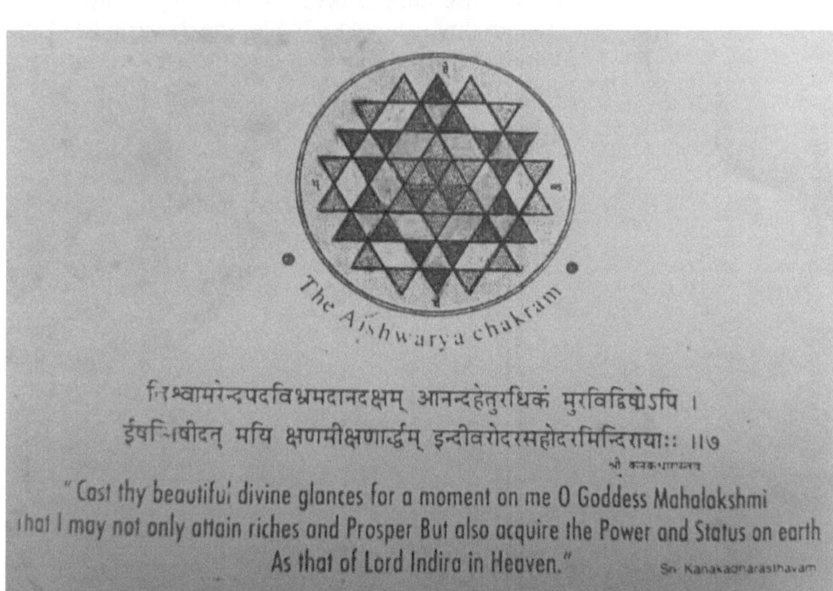
The Aishwarya chakram
विश्वामरेन्द्रपदविभ्रमदानदक्षम् आनन्दहेतुरधिकं मुरविद्विषोऽपि ।
ईषन्निषीदन् मयि क्षणमीक्षणार्द्धम् इन्दीवरोदरसहोदरमिन्दिरायाः ॥७
"Cast thy beautiful divine glances for a moment on me O Goddess Mahalakshmi
that I may not only attain riches and Prosper But also acquire the Power and Status on earth
As that of Lord Indira in Heaven."
Sri Kanakadharasthavam

Testimonials

I first discovered Guruji through his YouTube channel, where he generously shared the Maha Mandiram, a part of Kriya Yoga, in one of his videos, offering it without any commercial intention. He encouraged viewers to take his class if they experienced happiness or personal growth from practicing the Maha Mandiram.

Curious, I decided to try it for myself, and I was amazed by the inner peace and benefits of meditation that I felt. Motivated by this experience, I reached out to Guruji, asking for a personal class. Despite his busy schedule, he kindly agreed to teach me. During our session, Guruji provided a thorough theoretical explanation of Kriya Yoga, which was deeply enlightening, and then guided me through the practice itself.

After practicing, I truly felt the mental clarity and surge of inner energy he had promised. My thoughts and life began to feel more streamlined, and I could sense a profound shift within me. Guruji is deeply committed to sharing and teaching this powerful practice with others.

Before I began practicing Kriya Yoga, I was at a professional crossroads in the cinema industry. However, after consistently practicing Kriya Yoga daily, I had the opportunity to write a song for the movie Indian 2, and it became a hit.

– Pa. Vijay

Lyrisist

I work as a Dorn therapist, focusing on spine and foot reflexology. I used to feel tired easily and was searching for ways to boost my energy. One day, while exploring YouTube, I stumbled upon a video by Guruji that caught my attention. It inspired me to attend a Kriya Yoga class. That first class was such an incredible and unique experience that I decided to make Kriya Yoga a regular part of my life.

Now, after 3.5 years of consistent practice, I'm on my 19th Mandala. I've never felt this kind of energy before—Kriya Yoga is truly powerful. Since starting, my life has transformed in so many ways. My anger has significantly reduced, and I've gained more clarity and wisdom. For example, when I face challenges, I often sense the right solutions intuitively.

This journey has also sharpened my awareness of what is good for me and what isn't. I feel more confident in choosing the right paths, and it's had a positive impact on my work, family life, and overall self-confidence. Kriya Yoga has been a blessing, and I'm deeply grateful to have discovered it through God's grace.

– SM Arockia Leema

Dorn Therapist

Coimbatore

Hello everyone,

I have been practicing Kriya Yoga for the past two and a half years. Before I started, I often felt confused and struggled to make decisions in my life. However, as I continued practicing, I noticed a sense of calmness and balance developing within me.

This practice strengthened my faith in Kriya Yoga. My thoughts became clearer, my heart felt lighter, and my mind grew stronger. I also began to feel the blessings of divine energy guiding me. I gained confidence in my actions, and the quality of my work improved significantly.

I now fully engage in all activities with focus, and my success rate has steadily increased. Kriya Yoga also taught me to take responsibility for my circumstances and served as a valuable guide for moving forward in life.

I am deeply grateful to my Guru and the Universe for bringing this practice into my life.

With heartfelt thanks,

– Prakash

Coimbatore

My Experiences with Kriya Yoga

Greetings! I am from Salem. After working as an electrical engineer in the Electricity Board and later for the Dubai Government, I retired three years ago and have since been living in my hometown with my family.

I have been on a spiritual quest since the 1980s. Last year, I came across an interview on YouTube where Guruji spoke about "Siva Kriya Yoga." In the video, he explained Siva Kriya in a clear and detailed manner and even demonstrated the Bird Kriya.

The practices appeared very simple. When I learned about a one-day workshop in Erode on April 30, 2023, I immediately shared this with my wife. My wife, Mrs. Vennila, is generally interested in visiting temples and performing rituals at the home altar but had not shown much interest in pursuing a spiritual path. She had earlier mentioned that she might explore it after my retirement.

Recalling her words, I encouraged her to join me for the Erode workshop. From that day onwards, we have been practicing Kriya Yoga regularly, missing only a few weeks due to family commitments.

Consistent practice has brought me immense peace of mind and the ability to accept things as they come. I have developed a heart filled with love for all. I now clearly understand that I am solely responsible for both my successes and failures.

We have also been helping those in need through material support and food donations. Auspicious events have taken place in our family, and financial stability has started to improve. My temper is now under control.

Guruji's simplicity and kindness are truly inspiring. He guides us like one among us, patiently clarifying our doubts without any trace of anger. I am deeply grateful for his guidance.

I also bow with utmost respect to the five elements, the Siddhas, spiritual masters, countless yogis, and Mahavatar Babaji.

Let us all practice Kriya Yoga diligently every day and bring well-being to ourselves and the world!

Wishing you prosperity! Wishing the world well!

Guruve Saranam! Guruve Thunai!

– S. N. Ashokan

Retired Electrical Engineer, Salem

My name is Vennila, and I currently live in Salem. I am married and have two sons. Before Kriya Yoga entered my life, I should describe the kind of person I was. From a young age, under the guidance of my parents, I had faith in God. However, I never deeply thought about or followed the path of spiritual masters. Though I listened to many discourses, it didn't go beyond that.

On the other hand, my husband has always been deeply interested in spirituality. Since his childhood, he has explored various spiritual practices. After his retirement, as we spent more time together at home, we discovered Kriya Yoga through YouTube. Attracted to it, we attended our first workshop in Erode last year.

For the first time, I accepted someone as my Guru. Unlike ancient spiritual masters, Guruji was among us, living like one of us. He answered all our doubts, questions, and confusions with kindness and clarity. From that day, for the past one and a half years, my husband and I have been consistently practicing Kriya Yoga.

Even though we couldn't always attend live sessions with Guruji, we ensured to practice daily. This discipline has greatly improved my meditation and brought many positive changes to my life. Significant blessings have followed: my elder son's marriage and my younger son securing a good job. As a mother, there is no greater joy than seeing her children doing well in life.

The foundation for all these blessings is the practice Guruji taught us, the faith we had in it, and the commitment to follow it daily.

"Guruve Saranam."

– Vennila Ashokan

Salem

Guruve Saranam

Greetings to all!

My name is Sangavi, and I am a 10th-grade student at a government higher secondary school. In 2023, under my father's guidance, I learned Kriya Yoga. From that day onward, I started experiencing many positive changes in my life.

Through the practice of Kriya Yoga, my memory power has improved, and I have become the second-ranking student in my class. I also learned to control my anger, reduced feelings of jealousy, and overcame low self-esteem.

Now, I participate in all school events without any fear. Additionally, Kriya Yoga has brought happiness into my life.

Based on my experience, I encourage all school students like me to learn Kriya Yoga. Let's bring pride to our families and our nation while creating a significant transformation in ourselves.

I am deeply grateful to my Guru and the Universe for teaching me this sacred practice.

– Sangavi

Salutations to the Almighty and my Guruji Ayya!

My name is Visuvam, and I live in Kuttapalayam village in Erode district. In the year 2022, during the Maha Shivaratri festival, I learned Kriya Yoga. Since that day, I have been experiencing profound transformations in my life, my family, and my profession.

I found mental solutions to challenges that surrounded me—financial struggles, legal issues, and adversaries. Through these solutions, I have been achieving success.

Furthermore, I have taught Kriya Yoga to my wife, daughter, and son, and they too have reaped success through this prac-tice.

This precious treasure called Kriya Yoga will serve as a guiding light of success in everyone's life. My heartfelt gratitude and countless salutations to my Guruji Aiyya and the universe for introducing this to the world and attracting positivity into our lives!

– Visuvam

Hello Everyone,

I have been practicing Kriya Yoga for the past year. Before starting, I often felt confused and struggled to make decisions. But as I continued with the practice, I began to experience a sense of calm and balance within myself.

This practice has significantly strengthened my faith in Kriya Yoga. My thoughts have become clearer, my heart lighter, and my mind stronger. I also began to feel the blessings of divine energy guiding me, which gave me more confidence in my actions. As a result, the quality of my work has improved greatly.

Now, I approach all tasks with greater focus, and my success rate has steadily increased. Kriya Yoga has taught me to take responsibility for my circumstanc-es and has become an invaluable guide for navigating life's challenges.

Each day, after completing my Kriya Yoga practice, I feel energized with a profound strength and realization that Kriya Yoga can bring into one's life.

I wholeheartedly encourage everyone to embrace this practice and ex-perience its transformative power. Guruji's simplicity and kindness are truly inspiring. He patiently guides us, addressing our doubts with love and understanding, without any anger or frustration. I am deeply grateful for his guidance.

– Kavin

Field Officer

Poonachi

Hello Everyone,

I'm Ramanathan, and I've been working in the IT industry for 30 years. Today, I want to share how my life has changed since I started practicing Kriya.

After starting this practice, I feel a burst of energy that keeps me active all day. I no longer feel tired or unmotivated. My ability to focus has improved a lot, and now I can give my full attention to one task at a time. This has also made it easier for me to learn new things quickly.

Before practicing Kriya, I used to feel scared and unsure about the future. But now, those fears are gone, and I feel clear and confident.

Best regards,

– N. Ramanathan

IT Learning and Development Consultant

Bangalore

Greetings, Everyone,

I am Kalyana Sundaram from Madurai. On the auspicious day of Maha Shivaratri in 2023, I received Dheeksha and training in Kriya Yoga from our revered Kandhaguru Yuvaraj, at Bhavani.

I now practice Kriya Yoga daily for an hour during Brahma Mu-hurtham. This has brought immense benefits to my health, wealth, happiness, and prosperity. By practicing Kriya Yoga, one can achieve remarkable improvements in all aspects of life—not just in physical and mental well-being but also in longevity and even control over one's life journey, including its end.

Now, at the age of 70, I feel deeply grateful and happy. Every day, after completing my Kriya Yoga practice, I feel a surge of energy so powerful that I believe I could even lift a mountain. This is the immense strength and realization that Kriya Yoga can bring to one's life. I sincerely encourage everyone to embrace this practice and experience its transformative power.

Nandri, Nandri, Nandri. This too shall pass. May prosperity prevail.

– Kalyana Sundaram

Madurai

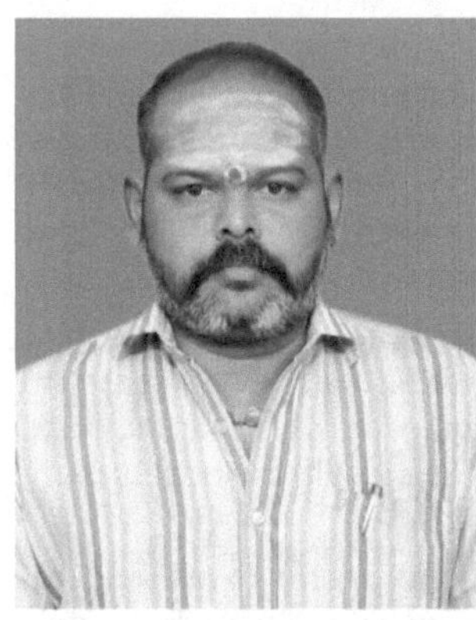

May love and grace prevail everywhere.

Kriya Yoga is the union of the body, mind, and life force. It is an extraordinary path that transcends the limits of ordinary knowledge. This idea resonates with the verse from Ayirami Anthadhi, which highlights that even at the age of 42, the wonders of divine grace are beyond measure. This grace is none other than the infinite compassion of Siddha masters.

Babaji, the embodiment of boundless mercy, stands as a guiding light in this Kali Yuga. His divine presence has uplifted countless souls, making yoga and spirituality flourish widely. Just as weak children require their mother's embrace, human minds today, prone to wavering and confusion, need the grace of Siddhas. Their austerities and teachings provide the path to liberation from such turmoil.

The divine searches for hearts willing to receive His limitless gifts. The term yoga itself signifies the unification of individual well-being with the cosmic consciousness. Siddhas, who have achieved perfection, live as embodiments of Kriya Yoga, fearlessly expressing the truth in their hearts. They possess the strength to convey wisdom without expectation or fear.

Among such realized souls, Shri Shimon Guru stands out as one who inspires and lives by these principles. His teachings on Kriya Yoga are beautifully captured in his works. I earnestly pray for his spiritual mission to flourish and for the divine Babaji to bless his endeavors abundantly.

With devotion, I also invoke the blessings of Lord Murugan of Thiruchendur, the eternal Pranava deity, for the success of this noble cause.

Yours sincerely,

– Trichy Balaji

Hello Everyone,

I have been practicing Kriya Yogam for almost a year and a half. Before I began this journey, I often felt confused and struggled to make decisions. However, as I continued the practice, I started to experience a sense of calm and balance that helped me connect with my inner self.

My thoughts have become clearer, and my heart and mind feel lighter and stronger. I have also started to sense the blessings of divine energy guiding me, which has increased my confidence in my actions. As a result, the quality of my work has significantly improved.

Now, I approach all tasks with greater focus, and my successes have steadily increased. Kriya Yogam has taught me to take responsibility for my circum-stances and has become an invaluable guide in navigating life's challenges.

Each day, after completing my Kriya Yogam practice, I feel energized with a profound sense of strength and understanding regarding the transformative power that Kriya Yoga can bring into one's life.

I wholeheartedly encourage everyone to embrace this practice and experience its benefits. Guruji's simplicity and kindness are truly inspiring. He patiently guides us, addressing our doubts with love and understanding, without anger or frustration. I am deeply grateful for his guidance.

– Navaneethakannan

Villupuram dist, Tamilnadu

Before I began my journey with Kriya, I often found myself feeling overwhelmed and confused by the challenges of everyday life. I struggled to retain information and frequently felt anxious, which made learning and focusing difficult. However, since incor-porating Kriya into my daily routine, I have experi-enced a remarkable transformation. I now enjoy a profound sense of calm and tranquility that has significantly reduced my stress levels.

Kriya has not only helped me find inner peace but has also enhanced my cognitive abilities. I have transitioned from being a slower learner to absorbing information more quickly and efficiently. My focus has improved tremendously, enabling me to approach my work with clarity and intention. As a result, I find myself feeling genuinely happy and content throughout the day, making my daily tasks not just manageable but enjoyable. This practice has truly been a game-changer in my life.

Shivaram

Bhavani

"Guruve Saranam, Guruve Thunai... (Seeking refuge and blessings from the Guru)

Greetings to all. I've been practicing Kriya for almost 6 month. The reason I started this practice was that my mind was filled with a lot of confusion and I couldn't make clear decisions. After working in the film industry for five years, I started my own business making foam mattresses and sofas. But I couldn't fully commit to it. That's when I met my Guru and sought his advice. Following his guidance, I began this Kriya practice.

For the past six months, I've been practicing Kriya and now my depression has vanished, there are no more problems in my family, and I can make decisions with a clear mind. The issues in my mind have started to decrease. My business is also doing well now. And I'm starting to see some opportunities coming my way in the film industry. I've realized that every human being should definitely undertake this Kriya practice. Today, I've truly understood this while being under the Guru's grace.

– Gautham & Co Shakthivel"

I first encountered Guruji's enlightening video on YouTube, which piqued my interest in Kriya Yoga. Intrigued by its promises of personal growth and inner peace, I decided to attend one of his classes. My experience has been nothing short of transformative.

Since I began practicing Kriya Yoga, I've noticed remarkable changes in various aspects of my life. For starters, I've seen a significant increase in my photog-raphy client base. I believe the clarity and focus I've gained through meditation have contributed to my creativity and ability to connect with clients on a deeper level, allowing me to capture their visions more effectively.

Additionally, the practice has helped me resolve ongoing family issues that previously weighed heavily on my mind. With the tools and techniques I've learned, I've fostered healthier communication within my family, leading to a much happier and harmonious home environment. The joy of being able to enjoy quality time with my loved ones is invaluable.

I sincerely encourage everyone seeking positive change and deeper connec-tions in their lives to consider attending Guruji's Kriya Yoga class. It's a journey worth taking, and the benefits are profound and life-enhancing

– Deva Chittar

Cinematographer

SRI KANDHAGURU FOUNDATION

211, Kandhaguru Garden , Koothampatti , Sanniyasipatti
Post , Bhavani (TK) , Erode (Dt) - 638311

+91 98420 23346 , +91 94423 54431 , +91 63850 40499

Email : srikandhagurufoundation@gmail.com

www.srikandhagurufoundation.org.in

Sri Kandhaguru

Sri Kandhaguru Foundation / MahaKriya Yogi Sri Kandhaguru

www.ingramcontent.com/pod-product-compliance
Lightning Source LLC
LaVergne TN
LVHW091313150826
845673LV00006B/1628

* 9 7 9 8 8 9 6 9 9 3 8 3 4 *